For ____

In search of Michael Dwyer

Enjoy the Read!

by

Chris Lawlor

Regards
Chris Lawlor
4/4/03.

First printed 2003

COVER PICTURES [Courtesy of the National Library of Ireland]

Front: "Michael Dwyer in St. Kevin's Cave", Chromolithograph from Irish Weekly Independent, December 1901.

Back: Wicklow 1798-1898 Centenary Membership Certificate, depicting Michael Dwyer's escape at Derrynamuck.

Printed by Leinster Leader Ltd., Naas, Co. Kildare.
Typesetting by Omega Typesetting, Newbridge, Co. Kildare.

CONTENTS

LIST OF ILLUSTRATIONS

DEDICATION

This book is dedicated to my wife, Margaret... by now an honorary Wicklow woman and always a fantastic inspiration and avid supporter of all my work on local history.

Thank you for everything.— Chris.

Preface

The extraordinary life story of Michael Dwyer has endured in the psyche of people within County Wicklow. Living, as I do, in the village of Dunlavin, I have grown up amid folk-memories of the heroic leader. In later years I continued to learn about Dwyer through the written word. This book is the first attempt to produce a small, compact but accurate biography of Dwyer in a single volume. It is based on the standard histories of 1798 and on the many excellent works concerning Dwyer and the events of 1798–1803 in County Wicklow. The book also draws on the folklore surrounding Dwyer and the lyrics of many ballads punctuate the text. Such ballads have kept Dwyer's memory alive and have played their part in etching the name of Michael Dwyer into the Wicklow psyche.

A number of people must be thanked at this stage. Firstly, a big "thank you" to my wife Margaret – a great help and support at all times. Thanks also go to my sons, Declan, Jason and Michael, all of whom showed an interest in this work and all of whom encouraged me to continue and complete the project. I hope you all read this book someday. You are the next generation of Wicklow men and I hope that my work will help to pass on the story of Michael Dwyer to your generation and to generations to come. I also wish to thank the Michael Dwyer Commemoration Committee of the Glen of Imaal for asking me to write this book and whose work on the new statue of Dwyer in the Glen of Imaal will provide a focal point within West Wicklow and will also help to perpetuate his memory in the area and beyond.

I wish to place on record my thanks to Ms. Joanne Finnegan of the National Library and to Dr. David Craig of the National Archives for permission to reproduce material in this book. Similarly, warm thanks also to the many courteous and helpful librarians including Ms. Penny Woods of the Russell Library, N.U.I., Maynooth, Mr. Shane Mawe of Trinity College Library, Mr. Mario Corrigan of Kildare County Library, Newbridge and Mrs. Margaret Birchall of Dunlavin Library. I also wish to express my gratitude to all the authors, publishers, companies and individuals who have permitted me to quote from their works. Such quotations from the already impressive corpus of knowledge on Michael Dwyer and the times he lived in can only enrich the present work. Thanks also to Katie Lowe's of Kiltegan and the Daynes family of Bluestone, Dunlavin for allowing me the use of photographs to illustrate the text. I am also indebted to Mairéad Evans of the Edenderry Historical Society, who proof-read my manuscript so expertly.

Finally, I hope that you, the reader, enjoy the book. I hope you find it interesting and informative. While adopting a double-sided approach to the subject by utilising both history and folklore sources, I have tried to be as concise and accurate as possible. Any mistakes in this volume are entirely my own fault, but I do hope that they won't detract from your enjoyment of it. This compact book is not the definitive life-story of Michael Dwyer; however I think that it will serve as a useful reference book and a good starting point for further study.

CHRIS LAWLOR January 2003

Introduction

WHEN the Michael Dwyer Commemoration Committee of the Glen of Imaal asked me to produce a pamphlet on the life of the famous Glensman, I was both surprised and honoured. When I began to think about the project before me, another feeling set in; a feeling that this has been all done before. Michael Dwyer's life has already been the subject of minute scrutiny by many excellent historians. Indeed, even the various phases of his life – his armed struggle against the authorities during the period 1798-1803, his term in Kilmainham Gaol and his later life in Australia – have been the subject of excellent individual works. In addition, the causes, course and consequences of the 1798 rising and its aftermath in County Wicklow have all been extremely well covered by various authors in many articles and books.

There was no point in re-inventing the wheel and I had no intention of doing so. The abundance of excellent secondary sources meant that my research could focus on them in an effort to collate the available material. What was missing, I felt, was one compact and handy volume which would give the general reader an overview of Dwyer's life and times. Michael Dwyer is larger than life. As well as being a historical figure, he is also a folk hero with a cult following. These twin facets of Dwyer led me to adopt a two-pronged approach when writing. As well as the large corpus of academic material which was available, I endeavoured to collect together various sources from the "popular history" surrounding Dwyer. This type of material is closer to folklore than to pure history, but I have tried to incorporate it in a way that does not compromise the historically accurate text. This little volume may operate at two levels and some readers may decide to look no further than the collected stories and ballads relating to Dwyer and his times. If taken, such a decision is perfectly valid, but I would hope that readers would peruse the text more closely in an effort to separate the man from the myth.

The mythic quality of Michael Dwyer is something that I have grown up with. In an article published in 1999, I stated that in the area covered by the parish of Dunlavin, Donard and Davidstown *Dwyer's memory is almost tangible.*[1] Some months later I received a letter from Co. Tipperary, part of which read: *"Dwyer's memory is almost tangible". Let me assure you that when I was growing up in the pre T.V. era it was actually tangible. My grandmother's accounts of the massacre in Dunlavin, Dwyer's stand at Doire na Muc and his many other daring deeds formed the patriotic philosophy and political opinions which I still hold to this very day.* This letter provides an excellent example of how powerful an influence the dramatic story of Dwyer's stout and prolonged resistance has had, both in Wicklow and far beyond its boundaries. One of my chapter endnotes refers to my national school history copy. This is deliberate and is another attempt to portray how the memory of Dwyer is ingrained in the local psyche.

At national level also, the name of Michael Dwyer is "up there with the best of them". A nineteenth century traditional ballad bears ample testimony to this fact.[2] The ballad is worded as follows:

THE THREE FLOWERS

One day when walking down a lane as night was drawing nigh
I met a colleen with three flowers and she more young than I.
"Saint Patrick bless you, dear," said I, "if you be quick and tell
The place where you did find those flowers – I seem to know them well."

She took and kissed the first flower once and sweetly said to me
"This flower I found in Wicklow hills, dew wet and pure", said she.
"Its name is Michael Dwyer – he's the bravest of them all
And I'll keep it fresh beside my breast, though all the world should fall."

She took and kissed the next flower twice and sweetly said to me
"This flower I found in Antrim fields outside Belfast", said she.
"The name I gave it is Wolfe Tone – the bravest flower of all
And I'll keep it fresh beside my breast, though all the world should fall."

She took and kissed the next flower trice and sweetly said to me
"This flower I found in Thomas Street, in Dublin fair", said she.
"Its name is Robert Emmet – the youngest of them all
And I'll keep it fresh beside my breast, though all the world should fall."

"Then Emmet, Dwyer and Tone I'll keep, for I do love them all
And I'll keep them fresh beside my breast, though all the world should fall."

This ballad is merely one example of how Dwyer, who was not a major United Irish leader before the 1798 rebellion although he worked his way up the chain of command somewhat during the conflict, was posthumously elevated to a status of leadership which he did not enjoy during his lifetime. Dwyer probably never saw Wolfe Tone, let alone met him. They moved in different circles. Unlike many of the leading figures within the United Irish organisation, Dwyer did not come from a well-to-do background. Well-known United Irish leaders such as Tone, the Sheares brothers and Lord Edward Fitzgerald had privileged upbringings. Dwyer, on the other hand, was a "man of the people" and it was precisely this quality that endeared his memory to the ordinary populace – the foot soldiers of Irish nationalism. Dwyer's innate intelligence ensured his rise through the ranks and, lacking formal education, the canny Dwyer more than made up for this fact by cultivating guerrilla survival skills which were second to none. While planning the abortive rising of 1803, Emmet and Dwyer met once or twice – literally! Perhaps the "uneducated" – but perceptive – Dwyer's opinion of the well-educated Emmet provides some insight into the minds of both men. Dwyer said of Emmet: *"If he had brain to his education, he'd be a fine man"*![3] Education, obviously, wasn't everything! In this ballad, the guerrilla leader of a tiny band of freedom fighters in the Wicklow Mountains is mentioned as an equal in the same breath as Tone, the "Father of Irish Republicanism" and Emmet, the "Darling of Erin". The heroic aura which surrounded Dwyer's stubborn resistance in Wicklow was utilised to the full by Nationalist Ireland's agenda both during his lifetime and after his death.

Nationalism needs heroes. In the summer of 1998 I attended a re-enactment of the battle of Derrynamuck in the beautiful and nowadays tranquil surroundings of the Glen of Imaal. One of the introductory speakers stated that Michael Dwyer could "deservedly take his place in any pantheon of heroes". He may have been correct in his assessment. Dwyer was much more than a mere outlaw. According to the evidence, he did not operate for personal gain.[4] He was politically aware and was engaged in revolutionary activities because he had a genuine political agenda.[5] Dwyer constantly hoped for another French invasion.[6] Despite limited contact with Emmet he knew about and supported the planned rising of 1803.[7] The five hundred guineas offered as a reward for taking Dwyer and the fact that any of his captured supporters were invariably charged with "rebellion" indicated just how seriously the authorities viewed this extraordinary man.[8]

The fact that Dwyer and his men were engaged in rebellion rather than banditry is an important one and is just one example of how the language used in connection with Dwyer's campaign, or any similar topic, can create for it a sense of legitimacy. Language can also detract from the legitimacy of any political or revolutionary cause. Prior to writing this pamphlet, it was suggested to me that the use of the word "rebel" should be avoided because Dwyer was actually a captain in the United Irish army. I have tried to use appropriate language in the text, but it is important to realise that ultimately it is the story told rather than the language used that really matters. Whether Dwyer is referred to as a "rebel", a "soldier" or a "freedom-fighter" and whether the scale of his operations constituted "battles" or "skirmishes" is really irrelevant to the overall story. Both battles and skirmishes result in the deaths of some of the participants and the cause for which they die regards such men as martyrs and patriots. These men become heroes and there was true heroism in the Wicklow Mountains at this time. The sacrifice of Sam McAllister's life at Derrynamuck in order that others might have a chance of survival was every bit as much an act of heroism as the sacrifice of Captain Oates' life for the same purpose during Scott's Antarctic expedition more than a century later. Both unselfish acts were inspirational and provided true instances of great gospel text *Greater love hath no man than this, that a man lay down his life for his friends.*[9] Acts of self-sacrifice such as Sam McAllister's are inspirational to any cause.

In writing this short biography of Dwyer I have not attempted to include all the information or all the stories told about his life. Tales such as the sea whistle incident,[10] Dwyer's shooting of the disabled informer "Danny the Bowl",[11] Dwyer's narrow escape by impersonating the mad Augustus Fitzgerald,[12] the escape from Rathdangan chapel[13] and many more remain untold. The approach used is selective and presents Dwyer's life in a "patchwork" format. Chapter one provides a sense of place with a brief examination of the Glen of Imaal area. Chapter two contains some necessary background information about the political situation in Ireland during the 1790s. Chapter three makes some brief observations about Dwyer's formative years in Imaal. Chapter four describes the "reign of terror" of late 1797 and early 1798. The severity of the terror in this area was one reason behind Dwyer's reluctance to end his campaign of resistance to the authorities. Chapter five examines Dwyer's role in the Wexford rebellion itself. Chapter six continues the examination of Dwyer's rebel activities during 1798, but the scene of the action has now switched to County Wicklow, as the Great Irish Rebellion reached its inevitable conclusion.

Chapter seven presents an overview of Dwyer's protracted guerrilla campaign in the Wicklow Mountains. Chapter eight refers to Dwyer's time in Kilmainham Gaol. Chapter nine provides a brief glimpse of Dwyer's "other life" as a settler in New South Wales, Australia, where he spent the final twenty years of his life.

Dwyer's exile and eventual death in Australia meant that the "Cult of Michael Dwyer" has also flourished in that great nation. Dwyer and the other members of the "Tellicherry Five" had many successors and transportation from Ireland in general, and Wicklow in particular, continued long after the 1798-1805 period.[14] Their descendants describe themselves as "political refugees".[15] The legacy of Dwyer and his successors has helped to shape modern Australia as a nation where the rights of the individual are respected and upheld; a nation in fact which values *the fundamental right of human freedom.*[16] Just as was the case in the folklore of Ireland, the myth of Michael Dwyer transcended his own time and place and in Australian folklore also Dwyer stands as a symbol for the "Rights of Man". The politically aware freedom fighter would have been pleased. The legend lives on.

NOTES

1. Chris Lawlor: "Unfinished Business" in *Dunlavin-Donard-Davidstown Parish Link,* Vol.V, No. 1, July 1999, p.6.
2. Website: http://www.dwyerclan.com/Three_Flowers.htm visited on 1/7/2002.
3. Charles Dickson: *The life of Michael Dwyer with some account of his companions*, Dublin, 1944, p.255.
4. Charles Dickson: *The life of Michael Dwyer with some account of his companions*, Dublin, 1944, p. 220.
5. Thomas Bartlett, "Masters of the mountains: the insurgent careers of Joseph Holt and Michael Dwyer, County Wicklow, 1798-1803", in Ken Hannigan and William Nolan (eds.), *Wicklow: History and Society*, Dublin 1994, p. 393.
6. Charles Dickson: *The life of Michael Dwyer with some account of his companions*, Dublin, 1944, p. 235.
7. Kieran Sheedy: *The Tellicherry Five*, Dublin 1997, p. 13.

8. Kieran Sheedy: *The Tellicherry Five*, Dublin 1997, p. 160. For charges of rebellion, refer to appendix two of this book.
9. New Testament, John 15:13.
10. Charles Dickson: *The life of Michael Dwyer with some account of his companions*, Dublin, 1944, p. 144.
11. John Thomas Campion: *Michael Dwyer or the insurgent captain of the Wicklow Mountains: A tale of the rising in 1798*, Glasgow, no date, p. 106.
12. Ruán O'Donnell: *Aftermath: Post-Rebellion Insurgency in Wicklow 1799-1803*, Dublin 1999, p.79.
13. Charles Dickson: *The life of Michael Dwyer with some account of his companions*, Dublin, 1944, p. 132.
14. Chris Lawlor: "From Wicklow to Woomera – Wicklow's Criminal Australian Connections" in *Dunlavin Festival of Arts Brochure*, XVI, Dunlavin, 1998, p. 23.
15. http://members.ozemail.com.au/~slaven01/mckeon/dwyer.html
16. Kieran Sheedy: *Upon the mercy of government*, Dublin 1988, p. 263 and Kieran Sheedy: *The Tellicherry Five*, Dublin 1997, p. 159.

Wild Imaal

ANY study of Michael Dwyer's exploits must begin with a look at the place in which they occurred. Dwyer operated throughout the Wicklow Mountains, but there is no doubt that both the homeland and the heartland of the rebel leader centred on the Glen of Imaal. This glen is located in West Wicklow and runs roughly east-west from the present Blessington-Baltinglass road (N81) to the western and northern slopes of Lugnaquilla mountain. The glen is drained by the youthful river Slaney and its tributaries. On the eastern side of Lugnaquilla lies Glenmalure, and the Glen of Imaal 'backs onto' this area. Both glens are very remote and both figured prominently as outposts of resistance to British rule in Ireland during different periods of history. During the late sixteenth century, for example, the Gaelic chieftain Fiach Mac Hugh O'Byrne carried out his military campaign from the fastnesses of Glenmalure, though he also used the Glen of Imaal as a channel of attack towards the plains of Kildare. This fact is referred to in stanza two of the song "Follow Me Up To Carlow": *See the swords of Glen Imayle, flashing o'er the English Pale, see all the children of the Gael, beneath O'Byrne's banners.*[1]

The Glen of Imaal forms part of both the Roman Catholic and the Church of Ireland parishes of Dunlavin. The Very Rev. Patrick O'Byrne P.P. wrote in 1926: *It was only recently that I was asked by a fine, respectable city curate whom I asked to pay me a visit, 'Where is the parish of Dunlavin?* Fr. O'Byrne goes on to answer this question by stating: *Geographically then, the parish of Dunlavin, entirely in West Wicklow, touches upon Hollywood, Ballymore-Eustace, Kilcullen and Narraghmore, and forms, to a great extent and for many miles, the North-Western boundary of Wicklow. We run along the Kildare frontier from Tober to Colbinstown.*[2] This description is very accurate, but it does not give us the full picture. The mouth of the Glen of Imaal opens out onto the lowland area adjoining the plains of County Kildare, but the head of the Glen of Imaal lies deep within the Wicklow Mountains and is impassable to traffic of any sort. This has numerous implications for life in the glen. East Wicklow, with its major towns of Arklow, Wicklow and Bray, is a world away from Imaal. The two sides of County Wicklow are poles apart.

Coupled with distance, the great mass of the Wicklow Mountains forms a physical "intervening obstacle" of the type referred to in the geographical "Push-Pull" model. Glenspeople are, even today, much more likely to work in (or move into) neighbouring Counties Dublin or Kildare than East Wicklow. It was even more likely to be the case in the late 18th century, when transport was confined to horse power or "Shank's Mare"! Life then was much more static. The ordinary people of the area, labourers and tenant farmers alike, did not move around nearly as much as people in these more mobile times. Wicklow's climate is another factor which hindered communications between the East and West of the county in the late 18th century. Snow and freezing conditions made the routeways through the mountains treacherous. We must also remember that the vast wilderness area of the mountains was much more exposed back then than it is nowadays. Most of the forest cover on the Wicklow range was not in existence in the latter half of the 18th century. The coniferous forests that dot the mountains nowadays are quite recent in origin.

This, however, is not to suggest that there were no routeways from West Wicklow across the mountains. There were roads (dirt tracks obviously) across both the Wicklow Gap and the Ballynabarnie gap (though not over the Sally Gap). The road system in the west of the county formed a good network, particularly below the 600-foot contour line or so. Robert Fraser's "General View of the County Wicklow" (1801) stated that the roads in County Wicklow were *uncommonly good.*[3]

Good roads or not, topography, distance and climate ensured that Glenspeople had more links to other towns in West Wicklow and in neighbouring Kildare than to any settlements on the Eastern side of the mountains. Baltinglass, Blessington, Naas and Newbridge all lie within a distance of ten to twenty miles from the glen. The strategic position of Dunlavin parish and its glen is hinted at in a letter from Mr. R. Nevill to Edward Cooke, the under-secretary, dated 10th December 1797: *We think it would be not only useful but necessary to have an officer and 20 men stationed at the village of Rathmore, it being the pass from the Blessington mountains to Dunlavin.*[4] Nevill obviously saw Dunlavin parish as an area to be watched and he had a good understanding of the topography of the district. Indeed, the authorities knew full well that the Glen of Imaal and Dunlavin parish held a vital geographical position. Dunlavin village was one of the garrison towns of West Wicklow in the 1790's.

Geographers nowadays refer to the concept of "region", and this concept is a vital one in the case of the Glen of Imaal. The glen is physically isolated from much of the surrounding area.

Using another geographical model, the Core-Periphery model, the Glen of Imaal is peripheral to larger towns (higher order centres) such as Baltinglass, Blessington, Naas and Newbridge. However, to get a true picture of the position of Imaal (even more so in the late eighteenth century, when regions were much more self sufficient than is the case nowadays), the core-periphery model must be turned on its head. To Glenspeople, Imaal is central. It would have been even more of a "central place"[5] in the 1790's. Now neighbouring villages become peripheral to the Imaal region itself.

Possibly the closest description of the Glen of Imaal as a distinct geographical region that I have ever come across is to be found in the Shearman Papers. Referring to the eviction of a number of Catholic families in the glen, Fr. John Francis Shearman wrote: *All this done in a remote glen of Wicklow in the year of grace 1862 – too remote to be reached by public opinion – a feeling well-nigh strangled in this region of serfdom.*[6] This extract indicates that Shearman viewed the glen as a separate entity; a place which outside influence and public opinion found difficult to penetrate. A later writer also noted that the Glen of Imaal and the Glenspeople were perceived as 'different' even within their

THE MICHAEL DWYER TRAIL

Visitors to the Glen of Imaal may follow the clearly defined "Michael Dwyer Trail". There are eleven stops along the way and each one represents a significant event in the life and military campaign of Michael Dwyer. Signposts such as this one have been erected to guide visitors along the trail.

own parish. Rev. Samuel Russell McGee had asked a resident of Dunlavin village about some Glenspeople who were approaching and was told *They're mountainy men; they're not like us.*[7] This indicated that the Glenspeople kept themselves to themselves. Their own perception of the upland-lowland divide within their parish only served to increase the social isolation of the upland parishioners.

One final fact worth noting about the position of the Glen of Imaal is that it was adjacent to one of the main roads to the South-East (i.e. the Carlow-Wexford region). This road followed a slightly different route in the late eighteenth and early nineteenth centuries. Before 1829 the back road to Tullow and Wexford diverged from the present Dublin road at Blessington and went through Ballymore-Eustace, Dunlavin and Stratford-on-Slaney, joining the road again at Saunder's Grove, *where traces of it could recently be seen entering the demesne from Manger Bridge.*[8] Despite this deviation, the Glen of Imaal was still close enough to one of the main routeways from the South-East to the capital. During the 1798 rebellion and in its protracted aftermath this road had to be held at all costs. Resistance to the authorities could not be, and was not, tolerated. The South-East was the epicentre of violence during the rebellion, and the authorities constantly feared a 'repeat performance' – another outbreak of rebellion in the South Wicklow-North Wexford area in the years immediately following the hostilities.

The Glen of Imaal is a transitional zone. At its mouth, it opens onto a lowland area which stretches across the plains of Kildare to the Hill of Allen. At its head, it offers a panoramic vista of the Wicklow Mountains with the summit of Lugnaquilla close by. The long, narrow morphology of the glen – following, as it does, the upper valley of the River Slaney – makes the area inaccessible from three sides. The topography also makes the area difficult to negotiate and the terrain itself is often rough underfoot. This physical isolation led to social isolation also. Not alone were Glenspeople perceived as different; they also perceived themselves as different. It was into this glen and its unique community that Michael Dwyer was born in 1772.[9]

NOTES

1. Pat Conway: *A pint of Irish ballads*, Ossian Publications, Cork 1993, p.13
2. Patrick O'Byrne: "West Wicklow" in *Souvenir Guide and Programme of the Imaal Bazaar and Fete,* Leinster Leader Ltd. Naas, 1926, p. 56. The station referred to was on the branch railway line to Tullow (now defunct).
3. Quoted in Charles Dickson: *The life of Michael Dwyer with some account of his companions*, Dublin, 1944. p.187
4. N.A.I. 620/33/139.
5. I use the term "Central Place" in the geographical sense of Christaller's Theory.
6. N.U.I. Maynooth Library, *Shearman Papers*, XVII, p.169.
7. Samuel Russell McGee: *Dunlavin, County Wicklow – A Retrospect*, Dublin 1935, p.14.
8. Claude Chavasse: *The Story of Baltinglass*, Kilkenny Journal Ltd. 1970. p. 62.
9. Charles Dickson: *The life of Michael Dwyer with some account of his companions*, Dublin, 1944, p. 22.

Troubled Times

LOCAL HISTORY involves at least two variables – place and time. It is local because it happened in a particular place – in this case the West Wicklow area. It is history because it happened at a particular time. Michael Dwyer's campaign in the Wicklow Mountains would never have happened without a build up of events beforehand, both at local and national level. There is a local history of national events, and Dwyer's campaign is one example of how an event can have vast local significance and yet be part of a much bigger national picture. To fully understand what happened in and around the Glen of Imaal, some knowledge of the general background is essential. However, this pamphlet is not a general history of either Ireland in the 1790s or of the 1798 rebellion itself. "The Year of Liberty"[1] is a good, in-depth study of the rebellion and "The 1798 Rebellion"[2] gives a good, brief overview in pamphlet form and is lavishly illustrated throughout.

The year 1798 is remembered as the year of the great Irish rebellion. The conflict was not confined to parts of Ulster, Wexford and Mayo, though certainly these areas saw some of the heaviest fighting. However, many areas of the country were affected – Timahoe camp in Co. Kildare, for example, held out against the authorities long after the Wexford rebels had been crushed. The whole rebellion came as something of a shock to the British authorities, who knew of the activities of the United Irishmen and who thought that they had averted a United Irishmen's revolution. Indeed, many United leaders were arrested before the rebellion, and in many places it was local rebels – with local figures to lead them – who were involved in the rising – hence the British surprise. The existence of the United Irish organisation was central to events in 1798 – both nationally and in the Glen of Imaal. The following extract from their "catechism" makes their aims abundantly clear: *Question: What have you got in your hand?* Answer: A green bough. *Question: Where did it first grow?* Answer: In America. *Question: Where did it bud?* Answer: In France. *Question:*

Where are you going to plant it? Answer: In the crown of Great Britain.[3]

Here, then, was an organisation that posed a threat to the British authorities, and all who were loyal to the British crown. It made reference to both the American War of Independence and the French Revolution. Both of these events were anathema to Great Britain and its monarchy. The American War of Independence threatened the very concepts of "Empire" and British "superiority" in an age of imperialism. The loss of the American colonies was the first real blow suffered by the British Empire, and it cut deeply. The colonies were gone, but at least they were three thousand miles away. Now Ireland, the island on Britain's doorstep, was showing separatist tendencies. British Loyalists (in Ireland as well as in Britain) were horrified. The French Revolution did not affect Britain as directly as the American one, in that they lost no land as a result of it. However, in its own way, the French revolution had an even more profound effect on British Loyalists because it threatened the very concept of Monarchy. Europe's *Ancien Regime* and the idea of the "Divine Right" of Monarchs were swept aside. The French were guilty of possibly the worst possible crime in Loyalist eyes – regicide. After all, who were Loyalists loyal to, if not the Monarch? Coupled with this, in the British case, the monarch was the head of the Anglican Church (in both England and Ireland). In Ireland, where the overwhelming majority of the population was Catholic, religious fears grew and added to the Loyalist anxiety about Republicanism rearing its ugly head in the form of the United Irishmen on the island that was Britain's neighbour.

In fact, by the 1790's, there had been comparative peace in Ireland for a century. The last military action of any note to have taken place on the island was the Jacobite-Williamite War, which ended in victory for the Protestant House of Orange. The eighteenth century had seen the introduction of the anti-Catholic penal laws which by the 1790s had fuelled both Catholic resentment and consequent Protestant fears. Generally the eighteenth century had been a peaceful one, although the odd violent incident did still occur, particularly in more remote areas like the Wicklow Mountains. A proclamation from 1715 informs us that: *a barbarous and bloody murder was committed on the body of Mr. Abraham Coats, in his dwelling house at Killinure, in the county of Wicklow, on Wednesday the seventh of December last, between nine and ten of the clock at night, by shooting the said Abraham Coats with a pistol, whereof he instantly died.* [4] However, such actions were rare and were probably the work of individuals. Even the so-called "Raparees" (or "Tories", from the Irish word "Tóraíocht" - "Pursuit", as they were pursued by law)[5] usually worked for themselves and were not motivated by any great patriotic drive! Raparees appeared in the 1690s after the Jacobite defeat and they survived in mountainous areas well into the next century. However, rural violence was rare in 1715, but by the 1790s the situation had changed.

Agrarian unrest, Republican ideas and continuing religious problems contributed to the melting pot that was Ireland in the 1790s. In October 1791, the society of United Irishmen was founded in Belfast and before its inaugural meeting on 18 October thirty-six members had already been secured; an additional six were elected on that occasion. Its objectives were to achieve a cordial union among all the people in Ireland, to bring about a radical reform of parliamentary representation, and to secure the inclusion in that reform of Irishmen of every religious persuasion.[6] However, as the 1790's wore on the organisation became much more radical, seeking to break the link with Britain altogether. By 1796 Wolfe Tone was aboard a French ship, one of Admiral Hoche's expedition. Bad weather prevented any French landing at Bantry Bay in 1796, but Tone had prepared an "Address to the People of Ireland" for the occasion, part of which stated: *The alternative which is now submitted to your choice, with regard to England, is, in one word, union or separation! You must determine, and that instantly, between slavery and independence; there is no third way.* [7]

Strong words indeed, and no doubt as to the threat posed to Loyalists! Predictably, in such a climate, Loyalists were uneasy. The Orange Order was founded in 1795, to counter the threat posed by a Catholic agrarian movement called the "Defenders". The Order, however, also opposed the United Irishmen. The appearance of a French fleet at Bantry came as a real shock to Loyalists (albeit a fleet which never landed). The French Republican threat was enough to ensure that Loyalists' attitudes hardened and after 1796 there was something of a hard-line Loyalist backlash against the Whigs (more liberal Loyalists). This led to a reign of terror being unleashed throughout much of Ulster and Leinster – including the Glen of Imaal – in late 1797 and early 1798. By the late 1790s, at national level, the stage was set for revolt, and in the Imaal area and its hinterland the scene was set for prolonged resistance.

NOTES

1. Thomas Pakenham: *The Year of Liberty* Granada Publishing Ltd. Panther Books Ltd., London, 1972.
2. Michael Kenny: *The 1798 Rebellion – photographs and memorabilia from the National Museum of Ireland,* Country House in association with the National Museum of Ireland, Dublin, 1996.
3. Thomas Pakenham: *The Year of Liberty* Granada Publishing Ltd. Panther Books Ltd., London, 1972, p. 206
4. Chris Lawlor, *The Massacre on Dunlavin Green – A Story of the 1798 Rebellion,* Naas 1998, p.17.
5. I am indebted to the late Br. Labhrás O Muircheartaigh of Naas C.B.S. for this piece of information.
6. Frank MacDermot: *Tone and his times,* Revised edition, Anvil Books, Tralee, 1968, p. 73.
7. Seán Cronin & Richard Roche: *Freedom the Wolfe Tone Way,* Anvil Books, Tralee, 1973, p. 196.

FROM BOY TO MAN

MICHAEL DWYER was born and raised a Glensman. His father, John Dwyer had married Mary Byrne of Cullentragh. [1] Michael was their eldest son. The family moved from the townland of Camara to the townland of Eadstown in 1784, when Michael was about twelve years old. Eadstown was not quite as remote as Camara, but it was still situated well within the Glen of Imaal. In the early nineteenth century Camara was *two thirds rocky and green pasture intermixed with heathy pasture with coarse grass through the heath; high and exposed with heath pasture on the mountain top.*[2] The move to Eadstown improved the Dwyer family's circumstances. John Dwyer was a farmer and the young Michael showed all the signs of following in his father's footsteps. Indeed, as Ireland was largely unaffected by the Industrial Revolution which had swept through parts of Britain in the late eighteenth century, there was little else for a young Glensman to aspire to as a means of livelihood. Land was life and working the land was vital to the tenant families in remote rural areas such as the Glen of Imaal.

Despite the long and laborious hours spent on the land, the young Michael Dwyer did receive some schooling. He could certainly read and write; letters written by him at the time of his captivity in Kilmainham Jail reveal a clearly legible and highly embellished script, with an accomplished knowledge of spelling and punctuation. The anti-Catholic penal laws meant that formal education was an undreamt-of luxury for Catholic children during the late eighteenth century, but Dwyer attended a type of "hedge school" run by Peter Burr. Burr was a Protestant graduate of Trinity College and he was a liberal and progressive thinker. [3] A schoolmaster named Birr (probably the same man) was a member of the United Irishmen and he later ran for election as a captain in the Imaal area.[4] Burr instilled a sense of patriotism, a love of Ireland and things Irish, into his students. Coupled with this, he instilled a sense of injustice regarding British rule in Ireland and hinted that the land of Ireland might be fought over again in future times. [5] The land tenure system also did much to nurture a sense of injustice in the small tenant farmers, who laboured long and hard on farms that could never be theirs, as the landlord system did not allow them to buy out their holdings. There was also a sectarian element in the area.[6] In the nineteenth century Catholic farmers in the Glen of Imaal were targeted for eviction as the Earl of Wicklow pursued a policy of populating the glen with protestant families. [7]

The Howard family held the title of "Earl of Wicklow" and they had extensive lands, not only in Wicklow, but also in Donegal. The Howards first came to Ireland in 1636. In 1667 Ralph Howard M.D. acquired estates in north Arklow and the Glen of Imaal. With them came Shelton Abbey, which would become the family residence. Although the Howards lived at Shelton Abbey near Arklow in east Wicklow; they retained a land agent in the Glen of Imaal. Later, in 1776, when Michael Dwyer was four years of age, another Ralph Howard was elected to the peerage as Baron Clonmore of Clonmore Castle, County Carlow. His daughter, Alice, inherited Castle Forward and its land in Donegal. The Howard family were respected members of the Ascendancy. They were also the principal landholders in the Glen of Imaal; in the early nineteenth century they held 2,330 acres of land in the glen, nearly four hundred acres more than the second largest landholders, the Hutchinsons.[8] In common with many others, Michael Dwyer, the son of a tenant farmer, found himself growing up in a landlord system which stifled the dreams and aspirations of those at the bottom of the landholding ladder.

The young Dwyer was supposedly a passionate lover of nature.[9] This is possibly very true, but it does not and cannot take away from the fact that Dwyer's youth was laced with hardship. The Glen of Imaal was a beautifully scenic area, but it was also a marginal one. About thirty five miles south west of Dublin, the glen was physically separated by the Wicklow Mountains from the more populated eastern parts of the county. It also offered a great contrast to the adjacent rich lowland areas of County Kildare. This reinforced its status as a distinct regional unit – an isolated outlier of county Wicklow.[10] The quality of much of the land in the glen was poor. Much of it was taken up with heath and bog, and some was too rocky for agriculture. The soils, particularly on the higher slopes, were acidic and soil erosion had exposed great granite outcrops in many places. The area experienced much orographic rainfall and much of the winter precipitation fell as snow. Given such conditions, life for a young Glensman was anything but easy.

There is a breed of dog known as the Glen of Imaal Terrier. Today, we are told that *this game little terrier comes from a wild Irish Glen, steeped in the romance of Irish History and legend. The Glen of Imaal Terrier dog was bred long and low to the ground with powerful head and legs bowed, this game little dog guarded their stock and fought many a fight for wagers away from the watchful eyes of the Law.* These terriers are *still well endowed with the characteristics with which they served their masters long ago in the mountains and glens of Wicklow.*[11] In a word, the Glen of Imaal Terrier was a hardy breed. This was also true of the Glenspeople. Dwyer's upbringing was hard; life was a struggle. There were bad years when the weather made survival precarious for a family of tenant farmers in a remote and infertile County Wicklow glen. The only break from the laborious existence of the tenant farmer came in the form of illicit gambling sports such as dog or cock fighting and in the consumption of alcohol in the cabins of the family or of the neighbours or in the shébeen. The young Dwyer was probably introduced to these pursuits from an early age. Such intervals were few and far between however, and everyday life centred on working the land. The long and difficult hours of physical toil 'toughened up' the young man though. On the eve of the 1798 rebellion he was about five feet ten inches in height, full-breasted and very straight in the back with a short neck and square shoulders. He had long legs and big feet, black hair and a dark complexion, large dark eyes, a short nose and a wide mouth with evenly spaced teeth.[12] According to his brother John, Michael was a "well-behaved, good natured young man; moral in his conduct, civil and obliging to his acquaintances and very true to his friends; by no means quarrelsome but always of a bold and daring disposition" [13] In his late twenties, Michael Dwyer too was 'hardy'. It was a trait that he would need and one which would serve him well in the long campaign ahead.

The young Dwyer's resoluteness was accentuated by a knowledge and belief about Imaal; a deep-felt "sense of place". The Germans have a word for it – "heimat". Loosely translated as "native place", heimat refers to more than the physical topography or even the cultural built landscape of one's own place – it also includes a unique sense of identity with the "local". This includes the culture, traditions, history, beliefs, lifestyle – the people's very hopes and fears, felt at the deepest level – as well as the place itself. In the case of Michael Dwyer from the Glen of Imaal, his feelings and emotions ran deep. This was the territory of the Uí Mail, a proud tribe who had provided at least three overkings of Leinster and who gave their name to Dwyer's native glen. He grew up amid the ruins of once-great civilisations. The remarkable abundance of prehistoric monuments in Imaal and West Wicklow generally marked out this place as having a long and noble tradition and history behind it. This area was settled even in pre-Celtic times, and the stone circles at Castleruddery and nearby Athgreany, the cairn atop Church Mountain and the majestic Brusselstown Ring on Spinan's hill formed the backdrop for the young Dwyer at play and at work. The landscape of West Wicklow was a living reminder of the glories of the past. In addition, the stories of heroic deeds and times gone by were etched into the mind of the boy from the glen by Peter Burr and by the folk tales, which were kept alive among the populace. Dwyer's "heimat" became a source of inspiration. This was his own place; these were his people. Dwyer retained the knowledge that he was at home in Imaal and its hinterland – it was the soldiers who were strangers in this place. Such thoughts would help to sustain him during the long guerrilla war that was yet to come.

NOTES

1. Charles Dickson: *The life of Michael Dwyer with some account of his companions*, Dublin, 1944, p. 22
2. Deirdre Heaney: *Land and Life in the Glen of Imaal 1830-1901*, Unpublished B.A. Thesis, N.U.I. Maynooth, p. 8.
3. Ruán O'Donnell: *The Rebellion in Wicklow 1798,* Dublin 1998, p. 69. See also John Thomas Campion: *Michael Dwyer or the insurgent captain of the Wicklow Mountains: A tale of the rising in 1798*, Glasgow, no date, p. 5.
4. Charles Dickson: *The life of Michael Dwyer with some account of his companions*, Dublin, 1944, p. 23.
5. John Thomas Campion*: Michael Dwyer or the insurgent captain of the Wicklow Mountains: A tale of the rising in 1798*, Glasgow, no date, p. 6.
6. N.U.I. Maynooth Library, *Shearman Papers*, XVII, p.169. Regarding the systematic evictions of Catholic farmers, Shearman wrote: *Should there be a man so daring as to raise his voice above the common herd he is set down as a turbulent spirit and entails on himself a persecution of the lowest and meanest character unworthy of the noble proprietors whose only excuse is that they act thus led only by the invidious whisperings of avaricious agents and their cowardly myrmidons.*
7. I realise that "Protestant" is a complex term, including many shades of opinion and belief. I use the term here to refer to members of the Church of Ireland and apologise to all who might take issue with the simplistic terminology but religious argument is not central to this pamphlet, so I hope that the content and context in which it is used is clear.
8. Deirdre Heaney: *Land and Life in the Glen of Imaal 1830-1901*, Unpublished B.A. Thesis, N.U.I. Maynooth, p. 10.
9. John Thomas Campion: *Michael Dwyer or the insurgent captain of the Wicklow Mountains: A tale of the rising in 1798*, Glasgow, no date, p.4.
10. Deirdre Heaney: *Land and Life in the Glen of Imaal 1830-1901*, Unpublished B.A. Thesis, N.U.I. Maynooth, p. 2. Heaney wrote: *The isolation from the more populous eastern parts of the county, where the county administration is based, naturally leads to a feeling that the area is somewhat of a backwater.*
11. Website – http://members.tripod.com/granitefields/new_page_3.htm – visited on 4/4/02
12. Charles Dickson: *The life of Michael Dwyer with some account of his companions*, Dublin, 1944, p. 24.
13. Elaine Hoxey and Caoimhin de Lion: *Michael Dwyer – Battle of Doire na Muc*, Donard, 1988, p. 4.

TERROR

THE threatened French invasion at Bantry Bay in December 1797 meant that the authorities in Ireland adopted a hard line with suspected members of the United Irish organisation. A reign of terror was unleashed and in 1797 that terror reached Dunlavin parish. The objects of the terror were the village blacksmiths of Dunlavin. Blacksmiths came in for particular persecution as suspected pike-makers – Owen Finn of Narraghmore, for example, was executed in 1798 and the Thomas Egan referred to here again narrowly escaped the hangman's noose on the day of the Dunlavin massacre (24 May 1798). A vivid account of the persecution of the blacksmiths read thus:

In the morning of the 20 October last [1797] between the hours of one and two, Lieutenant H____ of the Antrim Militia, Richard Fowler of Dunlavin and Thomas Butler of the County of Kildare went to the house of Michael Egan, and having broken open the door, desired him and his son Thomas Egan to come down out of their beds – they were not even allowed to dress themselves – and on the very instant that they appeared, they were knocked down and received many desperate stabs: naked and bleeding as they were, they were then conveyed to the guardhouse of Dunlavin, and on daring to complain of such treatment were again knocked down and beaten in a most unmerciful manner. On their arrival at the guardhouse, they were offered reward and to swear against thirteen [United] Irishmen, but on the solemn declaration of the father and the son that they had no connection with persons of that description, they were again stabbed with bayonets. After having nearly killed the father, they dragged the son to a private part of the guardhouse and by every kind of cruelty and torture they could invent endeavoured to extract information from him; when not receiving any (as the poor man had none to give) the barbarians a third time inflicted several wounds upon him. One of the party then used this remarkable expression 'I'll be damned but Barber (who was another of the Antrim Militia) has sharpened my sword very well, and with the next blow I'll take off his head.' They then left the son and went to the father, whom they used exactly in the same manner, and again returning to the son they said that since he would not give them any information they would hang him. To this they proceeded and, putting the rope around his neck, led him to the winding staircase where (again not being able to obtain information from a person who had none to give) Lieut. H____ ordered Mr. Causker, a corporal, to tie him up, which was instantly done – he was then turned off. They then threatened the father that they would kill him also if he would not inform; but at this time, a gentleman of profession, hearing the shrieks of the relatives of these miserable men, came to the window and prevailed on the barbarians to let Thomas Egan be cut down. He was then cut down, but not before he was entirely deprived of his senses. One would have imagined that an hospital or an infirmary would be the place to where the wretch would then have been conducted. No such thing. He was hurried to the gaol of Wicklow, where he was confined thirteen weeks and laden with the most heavy irons; but we understand he has sworn examinations against the persons concerned in the above horrid transactions. Michael Egan the father, a man upwards of seventy years of age is lying in his bed in a most helpless situation; his breast and shoulder bone broke; and even if he survives, will never be capable of benefiting either himself or his family.

We have taken particular pains to be informed of the sequel of the story of Michael and Thomas Egan, the father and son who underwent so barbarous and brutal a persecution in the village of Dunlavin in the County of Wicklow – being, as we have already stated, dragged from their beds in the dead hour of night: the father's bones broken by officers and yeomen; for to the immortal honour of the poor Irish soldiers, they refused to take part in the atrocity; whilst the son was hanged three times in the presence of his aged father, with every aggravating circumstance of barbarity – and this without any colour of legal authority whatsoever, but avowedly by the inhuman and illegal process of torture to extort accusations from the agony of the sufferers. Upon the son refusing a bribe, the father was violently beaten before his face. The young man was cut down senseless and lifeless, his tongue hanging out of his mouth, but was nevertheless kept several days in the guardhouse. In six days he was taken with his hands tied behind his back to Wicklow gaol, where he remained in most monstrous contempt and violation of the law in a dismal cell loaded with very heavy irons.

He was then brought up to the Quarter Sessions at Baltinglass and an indictment read to him charging him with having spoken seditious words. He was then remanded and not delivered until he gave bail in so extravagant a sum as £500. The words with which he was charged, we understand, were fitter to excite laughter than to excite any such prosecution. And upon his appearance at Baltinglass on Thursday last the prosecutor thought fit to quash his indictment; and Mr. Richard Fowler as a principal party was himself to bail upon the information of Michael Egan against him, and is to answer at the next assizes of Wicklow.[1]

The search was on for United Irishmen in West Wicklow. The first few months of 1798, were punctuated by violent incidents in the area. The fact that the enemy did not wear a uniform and lurked within the larger rural Catholic population only served to fuel Loyalist fears -understandably, as the Republicans were like spectres to them, and almost equally hard to capture! The military response (which caused even further resentment) was to clamp down even harder on the troubled countryside. In April 1798, the house of John Dwyer (a relative of Michael Dwyer), who lived in Seskin in the Glen of Imaal, was looted and burned by the military. The reign of terror had reached into the remote glen itself. John Dwyer was a suspected United Irish Baronial Delegate. Indeed he probably was a baronial delegate, as the *Imale district and that bordering on the Co. Kildare was represented by one of the O'Dwyers and a young man named Hayden, both of whom were shot afterwards in the massacre of Dunlavin.*[2] John Dwyer himself was brought to Dunlavin market house, one of the first prisoners interned there, where he remained in captivity for about a month, before being executed on the village green.[3]

Michael Dwyer had also joined the United Irishmen. The exact date of his enrolment in the organisation is uncertain, as is the identity of the person who administered the United oath. Certainly the United Irish movement was gaining strength daily in the West Wicklow area during the summer of 1797. In May of that year, the organisation was openly recruiting in Hollywood.[4] Throughout the summer of that year, a United Irish recruitment drive, spearheaded by William Putnam McCabe, took place across County Wicklow.[5] It is very probable that Dwyer joined the United ranks around this time.[6] Thus he was a member of the outlawed organisation during the reign of terror which was visited upon Dunlavin parish and the Glen of Imaal in late 1797 and early 1798. The situation deteriorated as tensions rose to boiling point and on 24 May 1798 the terror reached its height as the rebellion broke out in the West Wicklow area. A letter from Rev Christopher Robinson to Edward Cooke dated 29 May 1798 stated that: *About 9 a.m. on Thursday 24 May the rebellion broke out through the entire neighbourhood of Dunlavin, Ballitore, Baltinglass, Stratford on Slaney, Castle-dermot etc., and the men, women and children joined in procuring arms of all description. They sung horrible songs never before heard by any Loyalist to excite the rebellion.*[7]

As the rebellion broke in its full fury, the terror tactics of the government forces in West Wicklow also reached a new high. Fr. John Francis Shearman described the massacre on the fairgreen of Dunlavin in some detail. Shearman wrote in 1862, when *"the memory of these events, is still green in Dunlavin, but few unless one in my position could elicit much information on a subject always dangerous to touch in that locality"*. Shearman also gave the time of the massacre as about 8.06 a.m., so it could have acted as a spur to the outbreak of further rebellion.[8] However the surrounding area was already violent, as many loyalists had fled to the garrison town of Dunlavin for protection before the massacre occurred. [9] Shearman's account of *The Fusilade on Dunlavin Green* speaks for itself:

Some days before this savage execution Capt. Saunders of Saunders ' Grove near Stratford on Slaney reviewed his yeomen corps and announced that he knew by private information all who were "United Men" and told all those who were sworn as such to step forward. Many, believing he had certain information as to their movements, came forward. One man, Paddy Doyle who got a hint from Capt. Saunders' butler that his master had no certain knowledge as to their sentiments, except a suspicion of their loyalty. When his name was called he said, "It was only U.I. men now to come forward, and he was not one". The remainder took the hint and the Capt. was foiled. Those who so unintentionally betrayed themselves were pinioned and marched as prisoners to the market house of Dunlavin for confinement till their fate would be decided. Next day as Capt. William Ryves of the Rathsallagh corps of Yeomen was on the lookout for insurgents on the hill of Uske his horse was killed by a ball aimed at its rider.

Capt. Ryves got himself to safety, rode to Dunlavin and then it was determined to shoot the prisoners of the Saundersgrove corps and others of the Narraghmore yeomanry, in all 36 men. Next day, May 26th about 8.06 these unfortunate men were marched to the green, which is situated, on the rising land of the village of Dunlavin, at an elevation of more than 400 feet above sea level, commanding a most magnificent prospect. The men were placed in a hollow on the north side of the green midway between the last house of the street opposite Sparrowhouse road and the chapel. A platoon of the Ancient Britons stood on the higher ground on the south side of the Boherboy road and fired on the unfortunate men with dread effect. All fell together dead and dying. Of the 36 men a few were only wounded. After the first fusillade the Ancient Britons returned to the market house to complete their savagery by flogging and hanging other unfortunate prisoners to strike terror into those who were going to the market for rations etc.

On the green, when all was quiet and the men left for dead; their friends and sympathisers beholding the remains watching from behind the neighbouring fences, the soldier's wives came to rifle the bodies of the murdered men. One poor fellow who was only wounded; when he felt his watch being taken away made an effort to retain it, but in vain for the savage woman got up her husband who dispatched the unfortunate man by firing a pistol into his ear. Another man, Peter Prendergast, who was wounded in the belly so that his bowels protruded; lay as dead and offered no resistance to the plundering and escaped. Towards evening the bodies, which were not already carried away by their friends, were carried to Tournant cemetery and there buried in a large pit. Prendergast being found alive, a woman replaced the entrails and bound him up in her shawl and had him carried in security to [his] home where he recovered and lived to an advanced age. Some few persons still living have a vivid recollection of these cruel and savage times. One old man remembers going to the market with his father and saw men writhing in the agonies of death hanging between pillars of the market house. He tells of one event which he witnessed and which relieves the savagery of the scene. A man, John Martin, snatched a sword from one of the soldiers. He was dragged to the Market House, the sword taken and hanged up on a peg. The delinquent was let away at the intercession of a magistrate present. While this was pending a soldier's wife took the sword from the peg to cut the rope by which one Tomas Eagan, a blacksmith, was hanging and blowing in death's agony. He came to and found means to escape to Dublin.

A SECTARIAN WAR CRIME

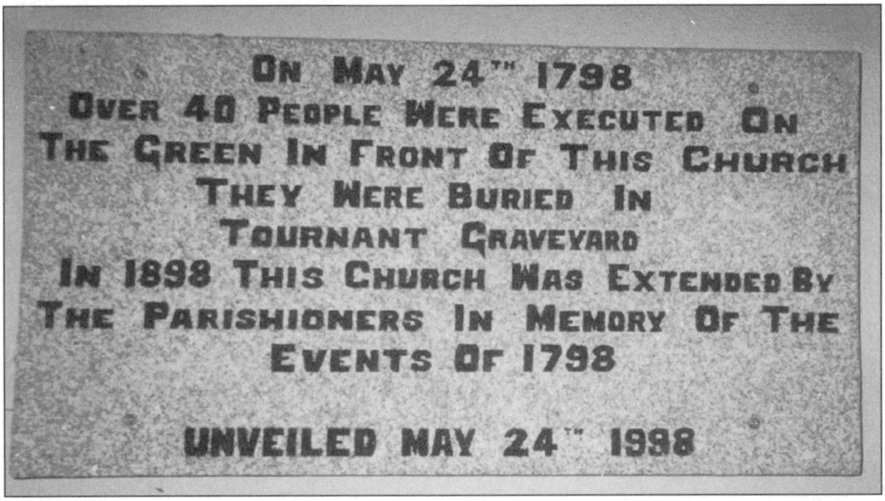

The site of the Dunlavin massacre on 24 May 1798 was carefully chosen. The corner of the fair green just outside the Roman Catholic place of worship was used to shoot the victims. The present Catholic church dates from 1815 but stands on the same site. This wall-plaque to commemorate the horrific event was put in place in the entrance hall of the church in 1998.

The Loyalist authorities had carried out a sustained campaign of "state terrorism" in the West Wicklow area.[10] The Dunlavin massacre was a horrific event and marked the zenith of the reign of terror in the region. The Dunlavin massacre was successful in preventing an attack on the village itself, but the resentment and bitterness that it engendered in the local populace spilled over into acts of violence. Indeed, the massacre at Dunlavin had repercussions as far away as Boolavogue, where news of the massacre had far reaching implications which sparked the Wexford rebellion.[11]

A distinction exists between the Dunlavin event and incidents in surrounding towns and villages. Other settlements had experienced violence and death too, but they had all seen some military action. Places like Naas, Narraghmore, Stratford-on-Slaney etc. had been the scenes of battles or skirmishes. In Ballymore-Eustace twelve executions had been carried out in direct retaliation for a rebel attack on the village. Dunlavin was different. What happened in Dunlavin was the shooting of disarmed and defenceless prisoners, suspects who had not been tried or given a chance to resign from the yeomanry, when no attack on the village had taken place. Perhaps it was a pre-emptive measure or perhaps there was a pre-conceived plot to shoot the men.[12] Either way, the incident in Dunlavin comes under the heading of "massacre" not "battle", "skirmish" or anything else.

As such, the Dunlavin massacre represents the first attempt at a policy of "ethnic cleansing" within the yeomanry. [13] This "ethnic cleansing" was not based on grounds of race or religion (at least one protestant was executed), but rather it was based on political views. West Wicklow was a politically aware and active area in the 1790's, and the policy which was implemented on Dunlavin green boiled down to the rooting out of United Irishmen, rebels, Republicans, French sympathisers, armed Catholics and any other feared category of yeomanry. Given the circumstances, the executions at Dunlavin, including that of John Dwyer of Seskin, affected Michael Dwyer deeply and the killings instilled in him a thirst for revenge which was left unsatisfied even in December 1803.[14]

The Dunlavin massacre was a watershed in the early days of the rebellion. It entrenched the views of both sides. It represented a "crossing of the Rubicon" by the authorities and many rebels regarded it as the event which pushed them beyond the point of no return. Michael Dwyer was one such figure: *Whatever might have been his previous determination, the arrest and ill-treatment of his father, the destruction of his cousins and neighbours in the slaughter in Dunlavin gave a fixity of purpose to that determination which could scarcely be relaxed.*[15] Dwyer's protracted military campaign against the authorities began on the day of the massacre on Dunlavin green – to be exact, when news of the massacre filtered through to the Glen of Imaal.

NOTES

1. Chris Lawlor: "Loose Ends from the Dunlavin Area 1797-1803" in *Dunlavin Festival of Arts Brochure*, XVIII, Naas 2000, pp. 20-22.
2. Charles Dickson: *The life of Michael Dwyer with some account of his companions*, Dublin, 1944, p.26.
3. Chris Lawlor, *The Massacre on Dunlavin Green – A Story of the 1798 Rebellion*, Naas 1998, p.60.
4. N.A.I. 620/30/89.
5. L.M. Cullen, "Politics and Rebellion – Wicklow in the 1790s" in Ken Hannigan and William Nolan (eds), *Wicklow: History and Society*, Dublin 1994, pp. 449 et seq.
6. Charles Dickson: *The life of Michael Dwyer with some account of his companions*, Dublin, 1944, p.25.
7. N.A.I. 620/37/211A.
8. Shearman Papers XVII reprinted in Chris Lawlor, "Dunlavin Green Revisited" in *Dunlavin-Donard-Davidstown Parish Link,* Vol. IV, No. 3, November 1998, pp. 6-7.
9. Chris Lawlor, *The Massacre on Dunlavin Green – A Story of the 1798 Rebellion*, Naas 1998, p.91.
10. Ruán O'Donnell, "Ultra-Loyalism in Wicklow: The case of the Dunlavin massacre" in *Wicklow Historical Society Journal,* Vol. 2, No. 4, May 1998, p.69.
11. Thomas Pakenham, *The Year of Liberty*, Panther Books, London 1972, pp. 169-170.
12. Chris Lawlor, *The Massacre on Dunlavin Green – A Story of the 1798 Rebellion*, Naas 1998, pp.108-115.
13. Chris Lawlor, *The Massacre on Dunlavin Green – A Story of the 1798 Rebellion*, Naas 1998, p. 123.
14. Ruán O'Donnell: *The Rebellion in Wicklow 1798,* Dublin 1998, p. 178.
15. Myles V. Ronan (ed.), *Insurgent Wicklow 1798*, Dublin 1948, p. 49.

DWYER AND THE WEXFORD REBELLION

IN MAY 1798 Michael Dwyer, though a member of the Wicklow United Irishmen, did not hold a position of seniority within the county organisation of the society. Dwyer was not implicated by informers operating in and around Stratford on Slaney in April, shortly before the outbreak of hostilities in West Wicklow.[1] Stratford was the scene of a battle on 24 May 1798, the same day as the Dunlavin massacre. The insurgent leaders at Stratford were Thomas Kavanagh and Martin Burke. Rebel losses were high and Thomas Kavanagh was executed.[2] Local folklore sometimes has it that Michael Dwyer fought in this battle, but this was not so. In fact, Dwyer was in hiding on the slopes of Lugnaquilla at the head of the Glen of Imaal during those crucial early days when the conflict started in the surrounding region.[3] Though not an elected officer within the United Irish network, the arrest of many senior figures such as Peter Hayden, John Dwyer of Seskin and the schoolmaster Peter Burr had thrust the more junior but up-and-coming figure of Michael Dwyer more into the limelight. Dwyer came to be viewed as an important organiser at local level and the attentions of the authorities forced him into hiding during the week preceding the outbreak of rebellion. Thus Dwyer was cut off from the earliest hostilities in West Wicklow and, although he undoubtedly received some accounts of events such as the Dunlavin massacre and the battle of Stratford, he may have been unaware of the existence of insurgent camps in the border areas of Counties Wicklow, Dublin and Kildare.[4] However, definite news of the defeat inflicted on Crown forces at Oulart Hill in County Wexford reached Dwyer on Tuesday 29 May.[5] On that day, Michael Dwyer decided to throw in his lot with the Wexford men and he set out for that county.

Dwyer's movements during the first week of June are something of a mystery. This in itself indicates that the Glensman was not a leading figure within the United Irishmen at this time. Had he been better known, or had he been a leading officer within the movement, his movements would have been noted and consequently would have been accurately traced. There is, however, no record of Dwyer having any command of significance in early June. Local tradition that he fought at Newtownbarry (Bunclody) on 1 June is probably inaccurate. He joined up with the united Wexford and Wicklow forces just north of Gorey at the end of May. Following a sojourn at Mountpleasant, he marched northwards with the army of North Wexford. He definitely fought in the battle of Arklow on Saturday 9 June, where he held a minor position, under such major leaders as Anthony Perry, Esmond Kyan and the Wicklow man, Billy Byrne of Ballymanus.[6] The Wicklow contingent in which Dwyer now fought was known as the Ballymanus division. During the battle of Arklow Dwyer's bravery was noted by the Wexford men.[7] Despite their bravery, the insurgents were halted at Arklow and fell back towards Gorey.

The battle of Arklow effectively stopped the spread of hostilities north of the County Wexford region. Following an action at Kilcavan Hill, Dwyer and the Ballymanus division reached Vinegar Hill on 20 June. This was the eve of what was to prove to be the decisive government victory of the campaign in the southeast. On 21 June, the rebel forces broke and the main body retreated towards Wexford town. Dwyer, however, did not go with them. Instead, he retreated northwards, rejoining some of his comrades on the way. They spent that night at Peppard's Castle and reached the sacked settlement of Aughrim on 24 June.[8] The survivors of Vinegar Hill began to regroup. Billy Byrne was no longer in command, but his older brother Garret now decided on an attack on Hacketstown, just over the Carlow border.

The battle of Hacketstown took place on 25 June. Actually, this was the second battle of Hacketstown.[9] The settlement had previously been attacked on 25 May. On the morning of 25 June the combined Wicklow and Wexford forces attacked the town, hoping to capture

HACKETSTOWN REMEMBERS

The 1798 monument in Hacketstown, Co. Carlow, which was erected in 1938 and re-dedicated on 28 June 1998. Hacketstown was the scene of Michael Dwyer's first significant command and he distinguished himself by his conspicuous bravery during the battle on Monday 25 June 1798.

arms and ammunition, which were both in short supply. It was at this battle that Michael Dwyer was given his first significant command as he led one of the flanking parties on that day.[10] The effectiveness of Dwyer's command over some of the men under him on the eve and the day of the battle of Hacketstown (especially those who had been drinking) has been questioned. It is possible that this point was made to distance Dwyer from atrocities such as murder and arson committed by drunken rebels.[11] Whatever the real situation regarding Dwyer's leadership qualities at the time of his first command, a determined loyalist resistance meant that the attackers' losses were high as the defenders picked them off from within stone buildings. Solid resistance from well armed forces within well-fortified positions amply demonstrated that, without cannon, the rebels could not hope to take such positions. Once again, Dwyer's courage was noted at Hacketstown. With two brothers named Laffan (Laphen) from Kilmuckridge, he managed to climb the barracks wall using scaling ladders.[12] Despite this gallant effort, the barracks proved too tough a nut to crack and the rebels eventually had to withdraw. Following a protracted engagement and the burning of nearly eighty houses, the deaths of Captain Hardy and eight loyalists were far outnumbered by losses on the attacking side.[13] One major loss to the rebel leadership was Michael Reynolds of Johnstown, near Naas, who had been very prominent in the battle that day.[14]

By late June, the great Irish revolution of 1798 was drawing inexorably toward its conclusion in the southeastern part of the country. There was a brief respite and a resounding rebel victory at Ballyellis on 30 June however. During this engagement, the Ancient Briton regiment from North Wales (who had been responsible for atrocities in the area of Newtownmountkennedy and had carried out the executions at Dunlavin) sustained losses of about thirty dead.[15] Michael Dwyer "took an active and prominent part in this action"[16] where he fought with Edward Roche, before chasing and killing a "huge Briton" when he "clove his head nearly in two with a captured sword".[17]

Although a resounding success, Ballyellis was not a major victory. Moreover, the rebel forces failed to pursue their advantage and nearby Carnew was not taken. Many ballads have been written about Dwyer, but most of them refer to his guerrilla activities during the post-1798 period. However one ballad, rather unusually, concentrated on the earlier part of Dwyer's career as a United Irishman and his involvement in the 1798 rising, mentioning a number of incidents in which Dwyer was involved, and it was published (with footnotes) in the late nineteenth century.[18]

ON CAPTAIN DWYER
Draw nigh, ye sons of liberty,
Come listen to my story,
It's truth to you I will relate,
It's of Hibernia's glory.

All in the chains of slavery,
Since Cromwell and his damned decree
Has robbed us of our liberty,
But now the time is over.

Now the time is drawing nigh
When we shall be delighted,
Those heroes brave on Wicklow plains,
So boldly and firmly United.

No Orange tyrants of the land,
Nor cavalry can them withstand,
They fly like chaff before the wind,
With dread in heart sincerely.

There is Captain Dwyer from Imail,
A stout true-hearted member,
That bloody twenty fourth of May (1)
He can very well remember.

Then the cavalry, like birds of prey,
Exulting in their tyranny,
And many a bleeding victim lay
Along the streets of Stratford.

This hero brave oft did declare
That he'd have full satisfaction,
As soon as he could well prepare
To join in warlike action.

But soon the boys, they did him join,
And Hacketstown surrounded,
With pike and gun they made them run
Their schemes were soon confounded.

Captain Byrne was there that day (2)
As stout as Alexander,
That Hardy and his troops knew well (3)
For shortly they were conquered.

To hear them bawl, to shout and run,
Crying out that they were now undone,
At every corner of the town
They were driven to destruction.

Those heroes brave, with loud huzzas,
Maintained the fight with valour;
The soldiers, to protect their lives,
Retired within their barrack.

But soon did Dwyer, with Holt and Neal (4)
And Reynolds too, that man of fame (5)
Set the town and barrack in a flame,
Which caused a deal of ruin.

The next attack was in Keadun bog (6)
When they met with Captain Dwyer,
One hundred cavalry and more
On him began to fire.

He and six more behaved so well,
The cavalry to their grief may tell,
You would laugh to see how many fell
And wallowed in the mire.

Out of six he lost but one,
Yet they were something hasty,
Of soldiers more than half a score,
He gave them much vexation.

To think how he had so much odds,
And they were hampered in the bogs,
Which made them curse and blame their Gods
That they had them forsaken.

There is a curse o'er Baltinglass,
And likewise o' er Dunlavin,
For spilling innocent blood thereon
Which is for vengeance calling.

Those vicious hearts that took delight
In deeds of blood both day and night,
But our heroes brave gave them a fright,
That their wits have them forsaken.

Now to conclude and make an end,
Let us fill up our glasses,
And drink to every daring man,
While time and season passes.

And steady in themselves, prepare
The green cockade once more to wear,
Drive tyrant villains to despair,
And that's our only glory.

(1) Dunlavin massacre and battle of Stratford.
(2) Garret Byrne of Ballymanus.
(3) Captain Thomas Hardy, Hacketstown yeomanry.
(4) Joseph Holt of Mullinaveigue near Roundwood – later transported to Australia and 'Big John' Neal-later an informer.
(5) Michael Reynolds of Johnstown near Naas, killed at the battle of Hacketstown.
(6) The battle of Keadeen, September 1798.

Despite the heroic imagery of this ballad, by July the tide of war had firmly turned in favour of the government forces. Retreat into the fastnesses of the Wicklow Mountains was now the only sensible option for the beleaguered rebel forces, but Michael Dwyer could scarcely have imagined just how long his resistance would last in these fastnesses as he and his comrades trekked towards Glenmalure in the first week of July 1798.

NOTES

1. Ruán O'Donnell: *The Rebellion in Wicklow 1798,* Dublin 1998, p. 69.
2. Wicklow County Council, *Wicklow commemorating 1798-1998: Calendar of Events,* p. 8.
3. Ruán O'Donnell: *The Rebellion in Wicklow 1798,* Dublin 1998, p. 165. See also Charles Dickson: *The life of Michael Dwyer with some account of his companions,* Dublin, 1944, p. 36.
4. Ruán O'Donnell: *The Rebellion in Wicklow 1798,* Dublin 1998, p. 165.
5. Charles Dickson: *The life of Michael Dwyer with some account of his companions,* Dublin, 1944, p. 36.
6. Pat Power, "The Battle of Arklow" in *Wicklow Historical Society Journal,* Vol. 2, No. 4, May 1998, p.24.

7. Charles Dickson: *The life of Michael Dwyer with some account of his companions*, Dublin, 1944, p. 38.
8. Charles Dickson: *The life of Michael Dwyer with some account of his companions*, Dublin, 1944, p. 38.
9. Carlow County Council/Carlow Urban District Council: *Carlow '98 Bicentenary Commemoration 1798-1998: Schedule of Events,* p.12
10. Wicklow County Council, *Wicklow commemorating 1798-1998: Calendar of Events*, p. 18.
11. Robert Duffy, *One hundred years too soon: Hacketstown and 1798*, Hacketstown Community Council, 1998, pp. 32-37
12. Robert Duffy, *One hundred years too soon: Hacketstown and 1798*, Hacketstown Community Council, 1998, pp. 42-43. See also Ruán O'Donnell: *The Rebellion in Wicklow 1798,* Dublin 1998, p. 251.
13. Wicklow County Council, *Wicklow commemorating 1798-1998: Calendar of Events*, p. 18.
14. Chris Lawlor, *The Massacre on Dunlavin Green – A Story of the 1798 Rebellion*, Naas 1998, p. 90.
15. I am indebted to Mr. Paul H. Haycock of Wigton, Cumbria, for this piece of information.
16. Charles Dickson: *The life of Michael Dwyer with some account of his companions*, Dublin, 1944, p. 44.
17. Charles Dickson: *The life of Michael Dwyer with some account of his companions*, Dublin, 1944, p. 45 and Ruán O'Donnell: *The Rebellion in Wicklow 1798,* Dublin 1998, p. 259.
18. R.R. Madden: *Literary Remains of the United Irishmen of 1798 and selections from other popular lyrics of their times*, Dublin, 1887, pp. 110-112.

THE END OF 1798

THE Wexford rebellion had failed and, although other parts of the island of Ireland saw further bloodshed later in that fateful year, the last chance of success for the United Irishmen died with their defeat in the southeastern theatre of war. Brief but false hopes flickered as rebel armies took to the field in Antrim, Down, Mayo and elsewhere. These hopes were crushed along with the armies that engendered them. Meanwhile, the remnants of the army of North Wexford, including Michael Dwyer and the surviving members of the Ballymanus division, had reached the relative safety of Glenmalure. There was now a council of war among the battered army's leaders. Debate raged about whether to stay in the shelter afforded by the remote glen or to move out of it and try to link up with other rebel forces elsewhere. One section of the army embarked on an expedition through Kildare and into Meath. The mastermind of the successful ambush at Ballyellis, Joseph Holt, accompanied this force, though it was against his better judgement. Dwyer and Miles Byrne of Monaseed remained in Glenmalure with a skeleton force, guarding the wounded.[1] Dwyer was responsible for the defence of the secluded valley at this time and he was referred to as "the Governor of Glenmalure".[2]

The Meath expedition was a fiasco. Following rebel defeats at Clonard and Rynville Hill, the majority of the force disbanded and only something between four hundred and a thousand rebels were left in the field in Wicklow.[3] Joseph Holt had been wounded twice and even had to feign death to escape with his life during the Meath debacle.[4] Following Holt's return to the Wicklow Mountains on 16 July, Dwyer rejoined the main army. At this stage the "general in chief" of the reduced force which remained in the mountains was Joseph Holt. Holt was a protestant from Redcross and his role in the Wicklow rebellion was rewritten and watered down by nineteenth century Catholic historians. One account tells us that there were men *far superior to Holt in the qualifications of a warrior.*[5] However, the truth was that

Holt was the *only surviving rebel leader of note willing to take command of the few hundred survivors in the Wicklow Mountains.*[6] The rebels' only hope of success lay in a successful French invasion, but Holt received news of the French General Humbert's surrender on 9 September.[7] Despite this, Holt continued to hold out, but the failure of the French and the onset of winter persuaded him to seek terms with the authorities. Joseph Holt surrendered, on his own terms, on 10 November – the day of Wolfe Tone's trial[8] – and the main body of the intrepid rebel army in the Wicklow Mountains disbanded.

Michael Dwyer had evacuated Glenmalure with the remainder of the insurgents on 6 August and on the next day they arrived in the Glen of Imaal. [9] Dwyer was home! The Glen of Imaal was geographically remote and the community within it was a close-knit one, which meant that Dwyer had many friends ready to shelter him locally. Even some elements of the yeomanry in this area were prepared to harbour Dwyer. [10] Here, in Imaal, he also had an extended web of kinship and could rely on the popular support which was one factor behind the longevity of his mountain campaign.[11] Knowledge of such support and shelter influenced Dwyer's decision not to avail of a protection which was offered to him in August. He may have even received such a protection, but not availed of it. He also feared becoming the target of a Loyalist reprisal attack.[12] A protection might be all very well, but with the memory of the Dunlavin massacre and other incidents fresh in Dwyer's mind, no doubt he may have felt that such a protection might not be worth the paper that it was written on. Dwyer considered the option of taking a protection, but ignored it and September saw him involved in the Battle of Keadeen (Kaigeen).[13] Dwyer and his men had decided to continue the fight. As the last stanza of the ballad "Dunlavin Green" implies, the Dunlavin massacre certainly meant that Michael Dwyer and his rebel band had many sympathisers in and around Dunlavin, Donard and the Glen of Imaal.[14] The executions on Dunlavin green and other acts of terror had set a chilling example and engendered much resentment among the local United Irishmen, and many inhabitants of the Imaal area were only too willing to give their support to Dwyer and his followers. This support was vital and all the more necessary following Holt's surrender in November, leaving the intrepid Dwyer as the only leader of note still at large in the Wicklow Mountains.

From this time onward, much of the information about Michael Dwyer becomes anecdotal. The great rebellion was over and the last remnants of Holt's fighting force had disappeared. Dwyer stood alone and his band of followers, though faithful, was very small. No more than fifteen men usually accompanied Dwyer.[15] Sometimes the number of followers was as low as three. Given these conditions and the overwhelming odds, many of the episodes relating to Dwyer concern his narrow escapes from the authorities. Early in December 1798, for example, Dwyer and some of his men attended a christening at Killalish, and their presence in the area became known to the authorities. They were sheltering in the house of the family of Peter Hayden (who had been shot in the Dunlavin Massacre), before they escaped over the mountain from the pursuing Highland regiment.[16] Dwyer and his men did still pose a threat to the forces of the crown however. On 8 December or thereabouts, there was an episode in the townland of Sruhaun. One account mentions that two yeomen named Magennis were shot because they were going to report Dwyer's whereabouts,[17] but it is more probable that they were shot because they refused to surrender their arms. Later that day, Dwyer's men also shot two other soldiers and a farmer named Young. The latter shooting happened at Tuckmill.[18]

Whatever the truth of the Sruhaun exchange, it proved that Dwyer still posed a threat to crown forces and their supporters in and around the Glen of Imaal. As the year 1798 drew to a close, many areas had been pacified by the authorities in the orgy of violence that followed in the wake of the attempted revolution. This bloody aftermath, coupled with the loss of life during the actual fighting meant that over thirty thousand fatalities resulted from the civil war that was the

BALTINGLASS REMEMBERS

This monument, erected in 1904, features the names of Michael Dwyer and Sam McAllister, but only one figure is depicted. Local oral tradition states that the statue is of McAllister and that Dwyer's figure was not included due to lingering bad feeling within Baltinglass concerning the killing of two local yeomen. Also, the statue was defaced by Black and Tans stationed at Baltinglass Union [Hospital] during the War of Independence. The right leg was broken but has been mended, while the top of the musket was snapped off and has never been replaced.

rebellion of 1798. Resistance had been crushed nearly everywhere, but the Wicklow mountains was a notable exception. As 1799 dawned, despite *very determined efforts to surround and capture him in the month of December 1798,*[19] Michael Dwyer from the Glen of Imaal, a captain of the United Irishmen, who had 'risen through the ranks' and gained in prominence during the rebellion itself, held out in that glen against all the might of the forces arrayed against him.

NOTES

1. Ruán O'Donnell: *The Rebellion in Wicklow 1798,* Dublin 1998, p. 277.
2. Charles Dickson: *The life of Michael Dwyer with some account of his companions,* Dublin, 1944, p. 47. Also Wicklow County Council, *Wicklow commemorating 1798-1998: Calendar of Events*, p. 19.
3. Myles V. Ronan (ed.), Insurgent Wicklow 1798, Dublin 1948, p. 49. Also Wicklow County Council, *Wicklow commemorating 1798-1998: Calendar of Events*, p. 20.
4. Ruán O'Donnell: *The Rebellion in Wicklow 1798,* Dublin 1998, p. 280. Also Wicklow County Council, *Wicklow commemorating 1798-1998: Calendar of Events*, p. 20.
5. Myles V. Ronan (ed.), *Insurgent Wicklow 1798*, Dublin 1948, p. 49.
6. Ruán O'Donnell: "The Rebellion of 1798 in County Wicklow" in Ken Hannigan and William Nolan (eds.), *Wicklow: History and Society*, Dublin 1994, p. 365.
7. Ruán O'Donnell: "The Rebellion of 1798 in County Wicklow" in Ken Hannigan and William Nolan (eds.), *Wicklow: History and Society*, Dublin 1994, p. 368.
8. Michael Kenny: *The 1798 Rebellion – Photographs and Memorabilia from the National Museum of Ireland*, Dublin 1996, p. 47.
9. Charles Dickson: *The life of Michael Dwyer with some account of his companions*, Dublin, 1944, p. 47.
10. Thomas Bartlett, "Masters of the mountains: the insurgent careers of Joseph Holt and Michael Dwyer, County Wicklow, 1798-1803", in Ken Hannigan and William Nolan (eds.), *Wicklow: History and Society*, Dublin 1994, p. 387.
11. Thomas Bartlett, "Masters of the mountains: the insurgent careers of Joseph Holt and Michael Dwyer, County Wicklow, 1798-1803", in Ken Hannigan and William Nolan (eds.), *Wicklow: History and Society*, Dublin 1994, p. 386.

12. Chris Lawlor, *The Massacre on Dunlavin Green – A Story of the 1798 Rebellion*, Naas 1998, p.126. Also Ruán O'Donnell: *The Rebellion in Wicklow 1798,* Dublin 1998, p. 296.
13. Charles Dickson: *The life of Michael Dwyer with some account of his companions*, Dublin, 1944, p. 78.
14. The standard form of the ballad ends thus: "Micky Dwyer in the mountains, to Saunders he owes a spleen, For his loyal brothers, who were shot on Dunlavin Green." See Chris Lawlor, *The Massacre on Dunlavin Green – A Story of the 1798 Rebellion*, Naas 1998, pp. 96-97.
15. Ruán O'Donnell: *The Rebellion in Wicklow 1798,* Dublin 1998, p. 340.
16. Chris Lawlor, *The Massacre on Dunlavin Green – A Story of the 1798 Rebellion*, Naas 1998, p. 127.
17. John Thomas Campion: *Michael Dwyer or the insurgent captain of the Wicklow Mountains: A tale of the rising in 1798*, Glasgow, no date, pp. 73-76. Interestingly, Campion entitled this chapter "Justifiable Homicide".
18. Charles Dickson: *The life of Michael Dwyer with some account of his companions*, Dublin, 1944, pp. 96-97. See also Ruán O'Donnell: *Aftermath: Post-Rebellion Insurgency in Wicklow 1799-1803,* Dublin 1999, p. 24.
19. Charles Dickson: *The life of Michael Dwyer with some account of his companions*, Dublin, 1944, p. 99.

GUERRILLA WARFARE

THE NEXT phase of Michael Dwyer's life was the one which established his renown. This renown has spread far and wide and has lasted over two centuries. The story of Dwyer's life up to and during 1798 is one of a young United Irishman who was drawn to the fighting in the Wexford theatre of operations, and who had taken refuge in the Wicklow Mountains when the crown forces gained the upper hand. Admittedly, Dwyer had shown conspicuous bravery during engagements with these crown forces such as those at Arklow, Hacketstown and Ballyellis. He had been given his own command and had stayed in the field even after the demise of Holt's contingent. Holt had laid down his arms in November 1798, but Dwyer continued his resistance until he gave himself up – on terms of his own choosing – in December 1803. In total, Dwyer continued his fight against the authorities for over five and a half years. The longevity of his campaign was staggering and his feat becomes all the more amazing when one considers the huge weight of odds stacked against him. Dwyer's guerrilla war has been well-documented elsewhere and this pamphlet does not seek to collate all the information concerning Dwyer's activities during this period. Instead, a selective approach has been adopted, making some general points and concentrating on the fact that Dwyer became a legend both in his own lifetime and afterwards.

At the outset, it is important to clarify that Dwyer was not a mere criminal or bandit. From late 1798 onwards *banditry and minor raids could continue as long as there were small numbers of unreconciled or outlawed rebels but this in itself could not be considered as insurrectionary warfare.*[1] However, Michael Dwyer had been a captain of the United Irish force. His family background was also entwined within the United Irish organisation. Many of his kinfolk had been deeply involved in the movement; for example John Dwyer of Seskin had been a baronial delegate.[2] Michael Dwyer's leadership qualities were noticed during the Wexford campaign and he had his own command from the time of the second battle of Hacketstown onwards. Hence Dwyer had a mandate for his actions from within the organisation to which he belonged.

One school of thought puts forward the argument that the United Irish forces formed the true Irish army of the time. The events of 1798 are thus viewed not as a rebellion, but as a war. This school of thought seems to need a legitimacy bestowed on what it would term "the martyrs of 1798". Therefore, the argument continues, the term "rebels" should not be applied to the soldiers of this properly constituted army who were fighting on the soil of their own land against forces loyal to an outside monarch. However, the application or non-application of the words "rebel" or "rebellion" is hardly relevant to the legitimacy or otherwise of the cause espoused by these men. The American Revolution, which is also referred to as the American War of Independence, also originated as a rebellion. Unlike the scenario in Ireland some twenty years later however, the American "rebels" won their "war" and were referred to as "the continental army". [3] The French "Revolution" was another example of a successful "rebellion". In Ireland the United Irishmen were truly "revolutionary" in their aims and aspirations, but their "rebellion" (a much bloodier affair than the French "Revolution" and the French reign of terror) ended in defeat. Language is strange, and perhaps it is important. Certainly it is important to modern political schools of thought, but the language of the events of 1798-1803 has come down to us through networks of both the victors and the vanquished. And, in the final analysis, language alone cannot bestow or withhold legitimacy on the organisations, events or people of the past. Informed opinion is aware of this fact.

Whatever view one takes about the legitimacy of the struggle, Michael Dwyer's status as a rebel leader was real enough. While small-scale operations were his principal modus operandi during the protracted guerrilla campaign, there was always the element of hitting out against the crown forces. Dwyer's operations were of necessity small-scale due to the dearth of numbers within his following. Moreover, any larger scale operations would have attracted the attention of the authorities and the very nature of guerrilla warfare involves small bands that hit both hard and fast before moving on rapidly. Such a campaign suited Dwyer, who was on home territory and whose *fieldcraft and survival skills were of the highest order.* [4] As the campaign progressed Dwyer (and, for a shorter time, Holt) became household names. They were actually far better known than many of the now more famous United Irishmen whose roles were re-appraised during the post-famine era.[5] Dwyer's exploits were well known during his own lifetime and news of his daring escapades only served to fuel the growth of his legend. He became a Romantic figure, *regarded as a criminal by the state, but considered a hero, champion, avenger and fighter for justice by the people among whom he sheltered.* A "social bandit" in the mould of Robin Hood, Michael Dwyer was *idealised and turned into a myth* who *never killed but in self-defence or just revenge.*[6]

The Romanticism associated with Michael Dwyer was both a cause and a consequence of the composition of a number of ballads about his life. Perhaps the most romantic (in every sense of the word) of these concerned the marriage of Dwyer to Mary Doyle, which took place on 16 October 1798, while Dwyer was "on the run" and avoiding the authorities.[7] Though certainly inaccurate, this ballad was later published[8] and it helped to establish and perpetuate Michael Dwyer's myth.

THE OUTLAW'S BRIDAL

As the torrent bounds down from the mountain,
Of cloud-helmed stormy Kaigeen,
And tosses, all tawny and foaming,
Through the still glen of lone Carrageen;

So dashed a bold rider of Wicklow,
With forty stout men in his train,
From the heart of the hills, where the spirit
Of Freedom has dared to remain!

Of grey frieze their caps and their surcoats:
Their carbines were close to their knee,
And their belts were well furnished with pistols,
Like men who knew how to be free!

Oh! grass-green the sash on their-shoulders,
Their caps crested green, with cockades;
And their leader he wore a long dagger -
The brightest and keenest of blades.

To the right ran Imale's lovely valley,
And before them was meadow and mound,
And the gallop of freemen was music
The echoes sprang out to resound!

Thou leader of horsemen! why hasten
So fleetly to Brusselstown hill?
What foemen, what yeomen await thee
To question, in Wicklow, thy will?

No foemen or yeomen they're seeking,
Though furiously onward they ride;
But their leader, he loves a young maiden,
And he's speeding to make her his bride!

"Halt!" Bridles were drawn, and they halted:
There's a farmstead looming ahead,
And the door of the dwelling is open;
Now the leader rode forward and said;

"There's somebody seeking thee, Mary;
A boy who came down from Kaigeen,
With forty brave bridesmen from Laragh,
With cockades and crosses of green!"

Oh! Mary came out in her beauty,
The loveliest maid of Imale;
The loveliest flower that blossomed
In all the wild haunts of the vale.

Arrayed in an emerald habit,
And the green and the white in her hair,
The Leader, he sprang from his courser,
As light as a hawk from the air.

He pressed her fair hand to his bosom;
She felt the big throb of his heart
"My Mary! I'll love thee forever,
'Till God on this earth will us part!"

They led out a horse on the heather;
She patted his neck with her hand,
Then sprang on his back like a feather,
And stood in the midst of the band!

The leader was soon in his saddle;
"Castle Ruddery's ruins!" he cried;
The priest's house is near to Green's river,
And here is the ring for my bride."

Away dashed the cavalcade fleetly,
By beauty and chivalry led,
With their carbines aflash in the sunlight,
And the saucy cockades on their head!

The priest he demurred and he pleaded –
The maiden she blushed and she frowned,
And the Leader of Forty felt nervous,
And tapped with his gun on the ground.

And thus went the parley, till even
Began to fall down on the glen,
And the priest thought a matron were better
To be 'mid such wild bearded men.

They were wedded: –"To horse!" cried the Leader,
And the bridal pair led the hot flight;
And away rode Dwyer, the Outlaw,
To his mountain-cave, back in the night!!!

THE RIVER SLANEY AT CASTLERUDDERY

The Slaney rises deep within the Wicklow Mountains and drains the Glen of Imaal beforre taking its leisurely course through the South-East of Ireland, eventually reaching the sea at Wexford. The lower banks of the Slaney saw much action during the 1798 rebellion and Dwyer's campaign ensured that the upper banks of the river were the scene of protracted resistance.

Ballads such as this presented Dwyer in a Romantic and attractive light. They were passed on from one generation to the next, forming part of an oral tradition regarding the leader and his exploits. There is no doubt that many of Michael Dwyer's exploits were hair-raising – the real stuff of which ballads were made. Narrow escapes such as the evasion of detection by assuming the disguise of a beggar man and boldly passing by the soldiers who were seeking him or lying across the rafters of Mangan's house while the yeomen searched the building at ground level [9] rank right up there with the legendary Robin Hood's entry into a hostile Nottingham in the garb of a butcher or his hiding in the branches of a tree as the sheriff's men passed beneath! Dwyer's most famous exploit during his guerrilla campaign was probably also his narrowest escape. This occurred at the cottage of Miley Connell in Derrynamuck (also referred to as Dernamuck and Doire na Muc) on the night of 15 February 1799. For once, Dwyer's lookout system had failed to alert him of approaching danger. Information received from a spy had led the military to the very door of Dwyer's refuge. Connell's cottage was the third in a clachan of three, situated at the end of an isolated boreen. The rebel occupants of the other two cottages had already been taken. Ned Lennon and Thomas Clerk surrendered at Hoxey's house and Wat McDonnell (McDaniel), Patrick Toole, John Ashe, John Mickle, Hugh Byrne and Darby Dunn were captured at the home of the Toole family. The military, a detachment of Scottish Highlanders led by Captain Roderick McDonald, surrounded Connell's cottage and called on the men inside – Michael Dwyer, Sam McAllister, Patrick Costello and John Savage – to surrender. [10] They refused and Costello and Savage were killed in the ensuing battle of Derrynamuck. Sam McAllister also lost his life, which he sacrificed in order to give Dwyer himself a chance to escape. Dwyer emerged from the cottage and *fled near naked and barefoot* before he *burst through the Scottish line* and *ran to freedom*.[11] The whole sense of the dramatic was enhanced because this event happened in the middle of a very cold winter with deep snow covering the ground. During

4/4/2003

Programme

• A word of welcome	Bill Walshe
• *Among the Wicklow Hills*	Davy Corrigan / Maureen Downey
• Michael Dwyer's early life	Bill Walshe
• *Dunlavin Green*	Liam Downey
• Speakers	Fr P. Finn / Rev. V. Kennerley
• Michael Dwyer in 1798	Bill Walshe
• Reading from the book	Breda Butterfield
• *Tin Whistle Solo*	Sarah Downey
• Speaker	Councillor Tommy Cullen
• *Wicklow Men of '98*	Maureen Downey
• Michael Dwyer's later life	Bill Walshe
• *Far Away in Australia*	Liam Downey
• Launch of Book	Joan Kavanagh
• Conclusion	Bill Walshe

Light refreshments to follow

A special thanks to all our musicians: Liam, Maureen and Sarah Downey, Seán Kennedy, Davy Corrigan, Nicky Kelly and Paddy McCormack

Thanks also to our hosts tonight for the use of their premises

Thanks to all of you for your support tonight

Chris Lawlor

DRIVE CAREFULLY AND SAFE HOME

his flight he *was lucky to slip on an icy patch as the bullets from a second volley whizzed past overhead.* [12] Dwyer was the only member of the rebel band to escape that night. The others were all either killed or captured. This incident inspired the best-known literary work about Dwyer, T.D. Sullivan's poem, "The Ballad of Michael Dwyer".

MICHAEL DWYER

At length brave Michael Dwyer and his undaunted men
Were scented o'er the mountains and tracked into the glen;
The stealthy soldiers followed, with ready blade and ball,
And swore to trap that outlaw that night in wild Emall.

They prowled around the valley, and towards the dawn of day
Discovered where the faithful and fearless heroes lay;
Around the little cottage they formed in a ring,
And called out: 'Michael Dwyer'! Surrender to the King!'

Thus answered Michael Dwyer: 'Into this house we came
Unasked by those who own it; they cannot be to blame;
Then let those guiltless people, unquestioned, pass you through,
And when they've passed in safety, I'll tell you what we'll do."

'Twas done. "And now,' says Dwyer 'your work you may begin;
You are a hundred outside – we're only four within;
We've heard your haughty summons, and this is our reply –
We're true United Irishmen – we'll fight until we die."

Then burst the war's red lightning, then poured the leaden rain;
The hills around re-echoed the thunder-peal again;
The soldiers falling round him brave Dwyer sees with pride,
But, ah! one gallant comrade is wounded by his side.

Yet there are three remaining, good battle still to do,
Their hands are strong and steady, their aim is quick and true;
But hark, that furious shouting the savage soldiers raise!
The house is fired around them! – the roof is in a blaze!

And brighter every moment the lurid flame arose,
And louder swelled the laughter and cheering of their foes;
Then spake the brave McAllister, the weak and wounded man –
'You can escape, my comrades, and this shall be your plan:

Place in my hands a musket, then lie upon the floor –
I'll stand before the soldiers, and open wide the door;
They'll pour into my bosom the fire of their array,
Then, while their guns are empty, dash through them and away!'

He stood before the foemen, revealed amidst the flame,
From out their levelled pieces the wished-for volley came;
Up sprang the three survivors for whom the hero died,
But only Michael Dwyer burst through the ranks outside.

He baffled his pursuers, who followed like the wind.
He swam the river Slaney, and left them far behind;
But many a scarlet soldier he promised soon would fall,
For those, his gallant comrades, who died in wild Emall.

There is no doubt that this ballad posthumously helped to enhance Dwyer's reputation and added to the myth. The name of Michael Dwyer is well-known beyond his native Wicklow, and this ballad is largely responsible for this fact. To many people, Dwyer is synonymous with Wicklow. Personally on at least four occasions in public houses I have had Dywer's name quoted to me with no prompting from myself other than to mention the fact that I hail from County Wicklow. For the record, the four instances happened in Doolin, Co. Clare; a crossroads pub near Dunmanway in west Cork; a hotel bar in Bayswater,

London and a "Rosie O'Grady's" in Midtown, Manhattan, New York City. The geographical diffusion of Dwyer's name and its association with County Wicklow is impressive! Thanks to T.D. Sullivan's ballad, Dwyer's escape from Derrynamuck is the first episode that springs to many people's minds when they hear his name.[13] Though Sullivan's ballad is the best-known example, it was not the only one to be written about the escape. Another ballad, published in 1887, refers to the same incident.[14]

ON AN ESCAPE OF DWYER

On a wintry night as the turgid stream
Rolled down the mountainside,
From the vault of heaven no star did gleam
And nought was heard beside,
But the rumbling roar of the mountain flood,
As it fretted into ire,
And deluged the cave where the outlaws stood
With their manly Captain Dwyer.
The noble hearted Dwyer.

Affection's fame ne'er warmed the blood
Of more devoted men;
Drenched by snow, by storm and flood,
They seek some friend to screen.
But they little know that the spy is on,
Nought can stay his foul desire,
And he tells in gold, each ounce, each dram,
Of the blood of Captain Dwyer.
Of the single hearted Dwyer.

Three friendly doors are opened wide
To aid the brave distressed,
Three pickets set and their arms are tried;

They take themselves to rest.
Through drifting snow and mountain storm,
O'er glen, through bog and mire,
In the dead of night the foeman comes
To seize on Captain Dwyer.
On the terror striking Dwyer.

The arrant Scot proposed a truce;
Oh, base and treacherous man,
But brave Dwyer threw back his overture
Saying 'We can die like men.
The innocent babes you will set free,
Their mother and their sire,
And all your vengeance heap on me,
I am the captain Dwyer.
My name is Michael Dwyer'.

But the kilted foes around them set
And fired the house of Connel
Those hungry Scots, the hound of death;
Ah, shame on you McDonnell
Spirits of the dead, the butchered of Glencoe,
Look down with vengeful ire
On you, degenerate sons, the murdering crew
That sought the life of Dwyer.
Of the freedom loving Dwyer.

The awful blaze ascends the sky,
Bullets quick are flying,
Within, there is blood, but no dismay;
Without the Scots are dying.
And there is no surrender from the few,
Not scared by balls, by wounds or fire,

Nor the blazing roof cannot subdue
The noble soul of Dwyer.
The lion hearted Dwyer.

The noblest deed in annal found,
And purest in devotion,
Sam McAlister receives a wound;
See that soul's emotion.
But the chieftain laid the foeman low,
In gasping death to expire,
His winding sheet's the drifting snow;
He fell by the hand of Dwyer.
By the unerring hand of Dwyer.

'I'll sell my life to save my friend'
Said the noblest blood of Ulster,
'I'll rush out and dare the Scottish fiends,
So perish Sam McAlister.
And then desperate fire they'll pour on me;
Then all I do require
Is to embrace that moment and be free,
My gallant Captain Dwyer.
Oppression's hater – Dwyer.

Then the manly chief, in softening mood,
Embraced his wounded friend,
'Oh no, for I'll fall with the brave and good
And so struggle till the end'
But rushing forth from the leader now,
The hero met their fire –
And purpled o'er the virgin snow
To save his captain Dwyer.
The persecuted Dwyer.

The furious Dwyer with vengeance strove
Against their whole array,
Disdaining death, he nobly stood,
And kept the Scots at bay.
Like goaded lion from his den,
Or tiger from his lair,
And beckoning on his last two men,
The true, the faithful Dwyer.
The vengeance vowing Dwyer.

Brave men, they fell and nobly bled
Among the gallant slain,
The name of Savage long will shed
Its memory o'er that plain;
And Costeloe, that brave young man,
The last to quit the fire
Was butchered by the unholy clan
As a vengeance on brave Dwyer.
The high priced head of Dwyer.

THE MYTH

This stipple print, entitled "The Wicklow Desperado", by John Martyn, was published in Walker's Hibernian magazine in November 1803, while Michael Dwyer was still active in the Wicklow Mountains. The cocked hat, the sword and the Republican cravat all add to the romanticism of the artist's imaginative portrayal of the folk-hero. [Picture courtesy of the National Library of Ireland]

A NATIONAL MONUMENT

The restored cottage of Miley Connell at Derrynamuck. This was the scene of Michael Dwyer's most famous escape and is situated on a boreen in a remote area deep within the Glen of Imaal. On 15 February 1799, Dwyer was lucky to escape with his life following an engagement with a detachment of Scottish Highlanders. The occupants of the cottage, Patrick Costello, John Savage and Sam McAllister were not so lucky that night.

After his eventful escape from Derrynamuck, Dwyer made for the house of Thaddeus Dwyer, who was a brother of the John Dwyer shot on Dunlavin green, and thence on to either Sleivecorragh or Corragh.[15] The prisoners taken at Derrynamuck were taken to Baltinglass, court-martialled and executed (except for Hugh Byrne who turned "Kings Evidence" and thus saved his life). Indeed Dwyer's continuing activities in the region meant that Baltinglass became something of a "court-martial capital" for the West Wicklow region.[16] Some examples illustrate this fact well. On 19 February 1799 Michael Doyle was tried under Captain Bellock of the Dumfries Light Dragoons and found guilty of "rebellion, robbery and murder".[17] He was sentenced to transportation for life. Doyle was perhaps lucky to be transported – on 9 March 1799 James Comyns was sentenced to death when he was found guilty of "rebellion and robbing Michael Fenton, a yeoman, of his arms and accoutrements and making for the hills with said articles".[18] A week or so later, on 13 March, John Byrns received the death penalty for "rebellion and carrying arms against His Majesty's forces".[19] On Christmas Eve 1800, a death warrant was drawn up for William Genoud following his capture, escape, re-capture and subsequent court martial on 22 December 1800.[20] It is both interesting and revealing to note that the charges against these men all mention rebellion rather than brigand-like outlaw activities. These primary sources reveal that at the time in question, many people, including the authorities, perceived that men such as Dwyer and his ilk were continuing the rebellion rather than engaging in mere banditry. Dwyer, like Holt before him, was conducting his campaign of orchestrated resistance precisely because he did have a political agenda and moreover, a specifically "United Irish" agenda, however ill defined it may have been.[21] Dwyer was engaged in violence, but as a politically aware rebel guerrilla fighter rather than as a mere cut-throat.

Dwyer's mountain campaign of guerrilla warfare would continue long after his escape from Derrynamuck in February 1799. Indeed, when Lord Cornwallis stated in a letter of 13 July 1798: "Our war is reduced to a predatory system in the mountains of Wicklow and the bogs of Kildare"[22] he surely could not have foreseen just how long Michael Dwyer and his followers would continue to hold out in the Wicklow Mountains. Dwyer was involved in many dangerous escapades, near misses and scary moments. News of such exploits endeared him to the public at large both during his lifetime and after his death. The ballad-writers were not idle and ballads concerning his wider activities rather than relating to a single incident were also composed. One such song is the work of Paddy Heany and Peadar Kearney (famous for our national anthem 'Amhrain na bhFiann'). This ballad is short on factual material but the heroic tone and rousing chorus mark it out as yet another work which added to the already famous legend of the rebel leader of the Wicklow Mountains.[23]

MICHAEL DWYER

Have you heard of Michael Dwyer and his mountain men?
Runs your blood like molten fire when you hear again
How he dashed like mountain torrent on his country's bitter foes
Like a thundering, tearing torrent on the craven yeos?
Chorus
Here's the chorus, chant it loudly on the still night air
As the war shout rises proudly o'er the trumpet's blare.
Chant it! Peal it! Till it echoes over every hill and glen:
Here's to gallant Michael Dwyer and his mountain men.

When the stars of freedom vanished and our flag went down
And the nation's hope was banished from each vale and town,
Borne intact through blood and fire, Ireland's banner waved again,
Held aloft by Michael Dwyer and his mountain men. *(Chorus).*

Still the nation's hopes are burning as they burned of yore
And the young and strong are yearning for the battle's roar,
But the blessed star of liberty shall never blaze again
Till we strike like Michael Dwyer and his mountain men. *(Chorus).*

Ballads such as these were vital because they ingrained Dwyer and his memory into popular culture. As noted already, Dwyer is synonymous with Wicklow in the minds of many people. He is also synonymous with the United Irish leadership. The fact that he was not one of the principal leaders during the main action of the rebellion in Wexford has been obscured by a nineteenth century revision of his role. The inclusion of Michael Dwyer in pictures of the United Irish leadership grouped around a table or in individual medallions on a plain background, the Romantic account of his resistance written by John Thomas Campion and, above all, the numerous ballads about his time in the Wicklow mountains have helped to etch the figure of Michael Dwyer into folk-memory far and wide. Dwyer's legend had been growing throughout his guerrilla campaign[24] and posthumous literary works would later elevate Dwyer to hero status. His prolonged resistance in the Wicklow Mountains had touched a communal nerve. Dwyer was more than an outlaw, more than a rebel, more than a guerrilla leader to many people. He was a symbol of hope at a time and in a place of oppression.[25] As he continued to elude capture, that symbol became brighter and the hope, instead of being dashed, grew in the breasts of an admiring public. Dwyer was a cause célebre in his day. To Republicans/Nationalists who had tasted defeat in the main rebellion, Dwyer's continued defiance burned like a beacon. Dwyer and his followers *gave pride and a sense of self-respect to those whose own hopes had been cruelly denied.*[26] As long as there was any hope, however slight, of another revolution or another French invasion, Dwyer would remain in his mountain lair and await developments.

As the years passed, hope of such developments faded. By 1803, the Treaty of Amiens of the previous year, though short-lived, had shattered any remaining hope of French intervention in Ireland. In July of that year, Robert Emmet's attempted revolution had petered out amid a mixture of incompetence and bad luck. [27] Meanwhile the net was tightening on Dwyer and his followers. The completion of the Military Road through the mountains was a major boost to the crown forces. This was possibly the first purpose-built road in Ireland – the purpose being to capture Dwyer and his band. Military barracks were occupied at strategic points along this road. There were garrisons stationed at Leitrim, Glencree, Seven Churches, Glenmalure and Aughavanna.[28] This new reality considerably hindered Dwyer's capacity for movement within the heart of the mountains. Coupled with this was the fact that the military had unleashed a campaign of arrests against known or suspected friends and relations of Dwyer. This strained Dwyer's kinship network almost to breaking point. The situation was very bleak for the remnants of Dwyer's pitifully small force as the winter of 1803 drew in. Without the kinship contacts, there was a lack of safe houses. Caves and other outdoor places of refuge such as abandoned mine workings were not suitable during a winter when snow lay several feet deep on the mountains. In this era of mini ice-age,[29] cold, damp and dreary conditions awaited the Dwyer faction as they faced into their sixth winter "on the run". With the changed political situation in France, the debacle that was Emmet's "flash-in-the-pan rising",[30] the large garrisons stationed along the new Military Road, a renewed military campaign against him which began on 10 December[31] and the absence of many of the arrested kin, Michael Dwyer's thoughts turned to the drawing up of terms of surrender.

SIGN OF THE TIMES

Today's visitor to the Wicklow Mountains may follow the well-signposted "Military Road". Completed in 1803, this road was built for the express purpose of curbing the military activities of Michael Dwyer and his men. Five military barracks were erected along this new road, and the county's infrastructure was significantly improved.

Like Joseph Holt before him, Michael Dwyer did not wish to surrender unconditionally. He made overtures via his wife to William Hume of Humewood. The commander of the military, General Beresford, wanted Dwyer to surrender "upon the mercy of government" (i.e. unconditionally) but Hume, while informing Dwyer that the actual surrender would have to be unconditional, certainly gave some assurances to Mary Dwyer.[32] The exact nature of these assurances, or at least of Hume's ability to honour them, is unclear. Certainly Dwyer's life was to be spared[33] and safe passage to America for four of his leading followers and himself was possibly agreed upon.[34] Dwyer may have been led to believe that he would obtain a full pardon on surrendering himself. [35] Whatever the truth of the situation, there is no doubt that the United Irish Captain Michael Dwyer laid down his arms on what he believed were his own terms when he walked through the gates of Humewood to meet with the Yeoman Captain and M.P. for County Wicklow, William Hoare Hume, on 14 December 1803,[36] thus bringing to an end the brilliant guerrilla campaign which had elevated him to the status of myth.

NOTES

1. Ruán O'Donnell: *The Rebellion in Wicklow 1798,* Dublin 1998, p. 340.
2. Chris Lawlor, *The Massacre on Dunlavin Green – A Story of the 1798 Rebellion,* Naas 1998, p. 59.
3. See for example: William Miller: *A New History of the United States*, London 1968, p. 104.
4. Thomas Bartlett, "Masters of the mountains: the insurgent careers of Joseph Holt and Michael Dwyer, County Wicklow, 1798-1803", in Ken Hannigan and William Nolan (eds.), *Wicklow: History and Society*, Dublin 1994, p. 388.
5. Ruán O'Donnell: *The Rebellion in Wicklow 1798,* Dublin 1998, p. 5.
6. Eric Hobsbawn quoted in Thomas Bartlett, "Masters of the mountains: the insurgent careers of Joseph Holt and Michael Dwyer, County Wicklow, 1798-1803", in Ken Hannigan and William Nolan (eds.), *Wicklow: History and Society*, Dublin 1994, p. 391. At this point reference to footnote 17 of the previous chapter is also suggested.
7. Charles Dickson: *The life of Michael Dwyer with some account of his companions*, Dublin, 1944, p.85.
8. John Thomas Campion*: Michael Dwyer or the insurgent captain of the Wicklow Mountains: A tale of the rising in 1798*, Glasgow, no date, pp. 16-18.
9. Elaine Hoxey and Caoimhin de Lion: *Michael Dwyer – Battle of Doire na Muc*, Donard, 1988, p. 13.

10. Charles Dickson: *The life of Michael Dwyer with some account of his companions*, Dublin, 1944, pp. 106-108.
11. Thomas Bartlett, "Masters of the mountains: the insurgent careers of Joseph Holt and Michael Dwyer, County Wicklow, 1798-1803", in Ken Hannigan and William Nolan (eds.), *Wicklow: History and Society*, Dublin 1994, p. 389.
12. The wording of this reference is taken from my sixth class history copy and was dictated to me by my teacher, Mr. Tom O'Neill in 1971. The copy is in the author's possession. The incident is verified in Thomas Bartlett: "Masters of the mountains: the insurgent careers of Joseph Holt and Michael Dwyer, County Wicklow, 1798-1803", in Ken Hannigan and William Nolan (eds.), *Wicklow: History and Society*, Dublin 1994, p. 389 and in Ruán O Donnell: *Exploring Wicklow's Rebel Past 1798-1803*, Wicklow 1998, pp. 30-31.
13. For example see: Kieran Sheedy: *Upon the mercy of government*, Dublin 1988, Foreword, p. 3. I am also indebted to Mr. Martin Miley of Fontstown, Athy, who has given me the words of another verse. This extra verse is inserted after the line: Then, while their guns are empty, dash through them and away! and reads as follows:

    Alone you shall not stand, brave Savage nobly said
    For alive I won't be taken, they can only take me dead.
    And says Costello "I'll stay behind and the last shot that I'll fire
    Will be at the man that bars the way of Captain Michael Dwyer".

14. R.R. Madden: *Literary Remains of the United Irishmen of 1798 and selections from other popular lyrics of their times*, Dublin, 1887, pp. 119-122.
15. Myles V. Ronan (ed.), *Insurgent Wicklow 1798*, Dublin 1948, p. 90 and Charles Dickson: *The life of Michael Dwyer with some account of his companions*, Dublin, 1944, pp. 110-111.
16. Chris Lawlor, *The Massacre on Dunlavin Green – A Story of the 1798 Rebellion*, Naas 1998, p. 129.
17. N.A.I. 620/17/30/6.
18. N.A.I. 620/17/30/10.
19. N.A.I. 620/17/13/15.
20. N.A.I. 620/17/22.
21. Thomas Bartlett, "Masters of the mountains: the insurgent careers of Joseph Holt and Michael Dwyer, County Wicklow, 1798-1803", in Ken Hannigan and William Nolan (eds.), *Wicklow: History and Society*, Dublin 1994, p. 393. See also Ruán O'Donnell: *Aftermath: Post-Rebellion Insurgency in Wicklow 1799-1803,* Dublin 1999, p. 101.

22. Letter quoted in Patrick C. Power: *The Courts Martial of 1798-99*, Carlow, 1997, p. 80.
23. Chris Lawlor: "Loose ends from the Dunlavin area 1797-1803" in *Dunlavin Festival of Arts Brochure*, XVIII, Dunlavin, 2000, pp. 20-28. The ballad is also featured on a website: http://www.linuxlots.com/~dunne/ireland/Michael_Dwyer.html visited on 8/2/2000.
24. Ruán O'Donnell: *Aftermath: Post-Rebellion Insurgency in Wicklow 1799-1803,* Dublin 1999, p. 79.
25. For an excellent overview of oppression and the general situation see L. M. Cullen: "Politics and Rebellion: Wicklow in the 1790s" in Ken Hannigan and William Nolan (eds.), *Wicklow: History and Society*, Dublin 1994, pp. 411-501.
26. Kieran Sheedy: *Upon the mercy of government*, Dublin 1988, p. 263.
27. Sean McMahon: *Robert Emmet*, Cork, 2001, p. 41.
28. *Freeman's Journal*, 3 March 1803.
29. Kieran Sheedy: *Upon the mercy of government*, Dublin 1988, p. 37. I am also indebted to Councillor Tommy Cullen of Blessington for information about climatic conditions at this time.
30. Sean McMahon: *Robert Emmet*, Cork, 2001, p.39.
31. Kieran Sheedy: *Upon the mercy of government*, Dublin 1988, p.43.
32. Kieran Sheedy: *Upon the mercy of government*, Dublin 1988, p.47. See also Ruán O'Donnell: *Aftermath: Post-Rebellion Insurgency in Wicklow 1799-1803,* Dublin 1999, p. 171.
33. Kieran Sheedy: *Upon the mercy of government*, Dublin 1988, p.47.
34. Wicklow County Council, *Wicklow commemorating 1798-1998: Calendar of Events*, p. 19.
35. Wicklow County Council, *Wicklow commemorating 1798-1998: Calendar of Events*, p. 19.
36. Myles V. Ronan (ed.), *Insurgent Wicklow 1798*, Dublin 1948, p. 124.

CONFINEMENT IN KILMAINHAM

FROM December 1803 to August 1805 Michael Dwyer remained a prisoner in Kilmainham Jail, Dublin, as did some of his men.[1] Unlike Holt, (whose surrender was supposedly unconditional, but, thanks to the intervention of the influential La Touche family among others, whose real terms of surrender were that he be allowed to go to Australia a free man)[2] Dwyer wanted to be shipped to the fledgling United States of America. Despite all previous assurances to the contrary however Dwyer was kept incarcerated at Kilmainham. Dwyer and his followers were committed to Kilmainham on a charge of high treason.[3] As state prisoners, they were not always satisfied with their treatment there. The following documents which were written to William Hume from Kilmainham by Michael Dwyer[4] and by Arthur Devlin[5] (one of his right hand men) testify to this fact:

Kilmainham, January 21st 1805

Dear Sir,

The high opinion that I always entertained of your honour and veracity induced me to surrender myself to the Government on your faith beyond that of any other gentleman of the County. The terms on which I surrendered you will be pleased to recollect. I am conscious that the violation of such terms in any manner is not with your consent or even privacy, and whereas such violation now had place, I think myself warranted in giving you an understanding through praying your enquiring into the nature of my complaints and if just your immediate remedy of them.

Agreeable to your promise I received very good treatment until the first of July 1804 (my over close confinement excepted) and which day I was ordered into the yard with the other prisoners. The allowance of tea, sugar, and spirits granted me theretofore was on said day entirely stopped from me by Dr. Trevor – after expostulating with Dr. Trevor

I requested of him not to deprive me of the spirits, as my health would suffer materially by being debarred of that to which I had been, necessarily, so long accustomed. All in vain, I was deprived of the entire. I was at same time debarred the company of my wife in such sort as to prevent my breakfasting or dining with her. Dr. Trevor told me that if I did not tacitly observe his orders, he would put me into that part of the prison intended for capital offenders. I told him that asking for the spirits usually allowed me did not warrant such treatment, which was so entirely opposite to the faith of Government pledged to me by the Honourable Mr. Hume, and therefore I said I would not go unless I was forced. He called Mr. Dunn to take me over to the place appointed. I went with the jailer quietly and peaceably, fearing if I had acted otherwise I would have done wrong, and in the mean incurred your displeasure. I remained there eleven days destitute of any maintenance other than the county allowance.

Agreeable to your instructions I wrote to your uncle complaining to him of my situation; he came accordingly and caused me to be brought from my cell to the jailer's parlour, where in presence of the jailer he examined me very minutely. He could find no charge against me – I asked the jailer in his presence if he could learn from his own knowledge of one, or from the reports of any of the turnkeys or attendants, that any conduct in any degree warranted ill treatment, he declared he never knew a more quiet or peaceable man, but said Dr. Trevor is a very passionate man, upon which your uncle said that for that purpose of easily releasing myself from the present difficulty, I should beg the Doctor's pardon. I observed to him how painful it would be to beg pardon when I had not given offence of any kind but, that however painful it was, I would comply as it was his wish, observed to him at same time that I had conducted myself in such sort as to give offence to no person, considering that if my conduct was otherwise, it would be forfeiting the friendship and protection of the gentleman unto whom I surrendered and offering him the greatest insult. I returned to my cell to wait the arrival of the Doctor unto whom I told I had been sufficiently punished and would be very much obliged to him if he would suffer me to go back to my wife and children. He said he would, and asked me if I considered that it was Hume's interposition obtained my return. I said I did not know, but was satisfied his interposition would redeem me from a worse place and greater difficulties. Dr. Trevor then told me he did not punish me for any crime or offence of mine, but as an example for the rest of the prisoners!!!

I was afterwards given to understand that Dr. Trevor had been assessing my character by often times saying I was a savage or tyrant unfit for any society. Upon my being informed hereof I told Dr. Trevor "your terms with me had been very much violated by such abuse", and he answered with an air of seeming disdain. "Your terms, your terms, I know what your terms are better than yourself. You have no terms at all. There is no robber or highwayman could make better possible terms than saving his life, and the capital offence is where you and such persons ought to be."

An investigation of the prisoners took place here some time after, before the Right Honourable Judges Downs and Day, unto whom I complained of the above treatment, which they seemed to disapprove very much and told Dr. Trevor it was highly improper, and said Dwyer's terms should not be by any means violated (to which lecture no attention was afterwards paid). I have never mentioned to Dr. Trevor what were my terms nor to any other person. Before the surrender of Arthur Devlin, Dr. Trevor said if he, Devlin, should surrender, Martin Burke's life should be saved and wrote a letter to that effect directed to Devlin which he received in Humewood. After his surrender such a letter was delivered to Burke's wife by the Doctor for Devlin. When Burke was afterwards sent for trial to Wicklow Dr. Trevor denied having held out any promise to him and said if Devlin had surrendered to him as he expected, and made terms for Burke as he had done with Hume, they should be treated well. Upon my mentioning to the Judges that Burke was sent for trial to Wicklow, they with astonishment asked me if Burke was hanged. I told them he was not and hoped he would never be hanged, whereas a gentleman had pledged his word for his safety. Judge Downs asked me who that gentleman was. I told him such promise was made to Arthur Devlin by Captain Hume at the surrender of said Devlin.

The above was declared by me upon oath before the Judges, and upon such declaration being made I desired Dr. Trevor should be called. I repeated the same before him upon oath, and desired that Dr. Trevor should be put to his oath, whereas he could in any respect contradict me. He declared upon his oath he believed I told the truth.

I now wish to know if such treatment is given to me and others who have surrendered to the government, on your faith, with your knowledge and concurrence. I am conscious it is not with your immediate knowledge or consent. I therefore, request your immediate enquiry into the nature of what I have herein related, and if you find upon minute enquiry that the above statement is true, I request immediate redress, agreeable to the implicit faith which I have placed in you.

I beg leave to remind you of the promises which you have made me, of your goodness, after my surrender, and hope you will by no means lose sight of them until you see them duly performed. I also return you my most sincere and grateful thanks for your kindness to me since the above period, and flatter myself with the assurance of a continuation of your protection and friendship.

I am, Honoured Sir,
Your most humble and obliged servant,
Michael Dwyer.

Although not as detailed or intricate, Devlin's letter to Hume followed much the same line of argument:

Kilmainham, January 9th 1805

Honoured Sir,

At the time of my surrender to the Government I had such implicit faith in your honour and veracity, as induced me not to have entertained the least doubt of seeing the conditions on which I had so surrendered faithfully observed and performed. On the contrary, scarce any of them is performed. My Uncle Bryan Devlin and family were to have been restored to liberty, but to the poor man's irretrievable loss he, his son and daughter still are detained close prisoners. I have been promised some clothes, but these were not conditioned for; it was your goodness to promise them, and I hope for the performance of your promise. I shall say nothing further of any complaint until I shall have the honour of seeing and telling you thereof in person.

We are given to understand that a major part of the prisoners are ordered to be liberated, all I believe except those who are conditionally predisposed of. I also think it would be time to dispose of me, life is not by any means worth enjoying on my present terms, there would be no sort of utility to government in keeping me here for a long time and then suffering me to transport myself out of his Majesty's Dominions.

I therefore wish it to be done speedily and hope you will press that business for me on such sort as that I may be sent quickly, or otherwise that you would cause me to be again restored to liberty, which if I professed in such sort as to be under apprehensions, I would certainly by my future conduct render myself worthy. I also beg of you, at all events to cause my Uncle and his family to be restored to liberty as agreed upon at the time of my surrender.

I am Honourable Sir with respect,
Your most humble and obliged servant,
Arthur Devlin.

William Hoare Hume, son of the Liberal Wicklow M.P. who was killed by rebels in a skirmish near Humewood on the 8th October 1798,[6] either following in the Whiggish tradition of his father, or because he was tired of being pestered (or both), did write to Dublin Castle regarding the imprisoned rebels. His letter made it clear that terms were sought from him and that he gave assurances to the surrendering men. However, the letter merely stated that they would be sent "out of the kingdom", so it is uncertain whether he actually agreed to grant them passage to the United States. Hume's powers to grant such terms to Dwyer and his group were always suspect anyway. However, Hume argued, shipping the men out of Ireland would calm the situation in Wicklow and Dwyer's sympathisers would be deprived of their figurehead.[7]

Humewood
February 19th 1805.

My Dear Sir,

There is scarcely a day passes that I am not tormented with letters or messages from those fellows in Kilmainham, who surrendered themselves to me – viz. Dwyer, Arthur Devlin and Hugh Byrne, complaining of ill treatment, of being almost naked, with various other complaints, and yesterday Dwyer's wife came here to tell me that she and her children had been turned out of the prison and that he was thrown into that part allocated for felons and put on the jail allowance and as she says without cause, which I am certain is not the fact.

But although I know there is no punishment too severe for them, yet it places me in a very awkward and unpleasant situation in this country to have these complaints made (however unfounded) that the terms I promised them to induce their surrender are not kept. It is now near fourteen months, I believe, since they surrendered. Is there any use in keeping them longer? If not, I must earnestly request that they may be sent off as soon as possible; for as long as they are kept in Kilmainham, I shall be tormented by them.

At the time they surrendered, you were in England. I told Mr. Wickham the terms I agreed to on their surrender which was that they should be sent off out of the Kingdom as soon as possible and that in the meantime they should not be ill treated in prison, that their relations who were confined merely on their accounts should be liberated, and that Dwyer's wife and children should be allowed to remain with him while in prison and sent along with him, and I assure you it cannot be of any service to this country, to have her at large here now. I therefore request that she may be confined again with her husband in Kilmainham, that is, if something very particular has not occurred to prevent it that I know nothing of at present. I enclose you some of letters they have sent me lately.

I am my Dear Sir
Yours most faithfully,
William Hoare Hume.

THE MAN

This engraving of Michael Dwyer (by T. W. Huffam after a painting done by James Petrie during Dwyer's time in Kilmainham Gaol) represents the only known life portrait of the "Wicklow Chief". Witnesses who had known the leader in person all agreed that it represented a very good likeness. [Picture courtesy of the National Library of Ireland]

While providing an idea of conditions in the prison and giving a flavour of Dwyer's well-documented[8] and long-running battle with Dr. Trevor of Kilmainham Gaol these letters also demonstrate that Hume did agree to terms with Dwyer and his men. However, unlike

Holt, Michael Dwyer did not end up in the place that he had expected. This was yet another factor in the growth of Dwyer's legend. The authorities were portrayed as "base knaves" who had failed to keep their promises. For nineteenth century nationalist historians this was yet another example in a litany of deceit on the part of the crown forces. The mythic qualities of Michael Dwyer were heightened by a sense of injustice at the treatment meted out to him. Hume's letter above hinted at a sense of disquiet among the people during Dwyer's lengthy time in prison. This disquiet developed into an outbreak of righteous indignation among Dwyer's adoring public following his departure for Australia. This phenomenon of support for the wronged leader continued posthumously and in its turn helped to sustain the cult of Dwyer in both Ireland and Australia. Before he sailed, Dwyer had gotten wind of his destination, and he protested vigorously. Once again he desperately tried to contact Hume.[9]

Sir,

As I don't know where to direct to your nephew, Mr. H. Hume Esq. and as you were pleased to say, that any terms which were made with me, you would see fulfilled, in his absence, I therefore call on you as a gentleman of Honour and Humanity to stand forth and save me from the effects of a flagrant breach of my conditions.

A very short time ago Dr. Trevor told me I should be sent away, and that not to America. I was alarmed and wrote to Mr. W. H. Hume twice but received no answer.

This day Dr. Trevor told me and the others who surrendered to Mr. Hume, to hold ourselves in readiness for that we should immediately be sent to Botany Bay, a ship being now ready. This communication, he declared, was by order of Government. Now Sir, my terms, which you well know, was to be sent to America, and my wife and children furnished with a comfortable passage along with me. But what is now attempted to be done? My solemn conditions are to be violated, the Sacred Honour of Mr. Hume is set at nought, and my wife and children are to be left without the smallest means of living or protection. This is such a terrible dereliction of everything which, even in uncivilized life, is held sacred that I know not what to do. The only thing which strikes me, is that you'll be so good as to exert your power on my behalf and that of the injured honour of your nephew.

May I request the honour of a visit from you as soon as possible and may I hope that I may not be the cause of attaching disgrace on the name of Hume, a family who hath heretofore been distinguished for their strict adherence to every principle of honour, as any breach of faith with me, will surely be published to the world.

I again humbly request a speedy answer, and the favour of a visit. Mr. W. Hume also said that I should not be removed without his acquainting my father. Your goodness will excuse my earnestness and attribute it to the unhappy circumstances which oppress.

Your very humble and obedient servant,
Michael Dwyer.
Kilmainham Prison May 12th 1805.

Despite this last minute appeal, Michael Dwyer's captivity in Ireland finished in August 1805, when, in company with his wife Mary, his cousin Hugh "Vesty" Byrne, Byrne's wife Rachael and their children, Arthur Devlin, Martin Burke and John Mernagh, the leader from the Glen of Imaal boarded the *Tellicherry* at Cobh, bound for Botany Bay. [10] So the process of ridding West Wicklow of United Irishmen, which had started on 24th May 1798 with the executions on the fairgreen of Dunlavin finally ended on the 28th August 1805 when the "Tellicherry" sailed for Port Jackson in New South Wales, Australia.

NOTES

1. Chris Lawlor, *The Massacre on Dunlavin Green – A Story of the 1798 Rebellion*, Naas 1998, p. 139.
2. Thomas Bartlett, "Masters of the mountains: the insurgent careers of Joseph Holt and Michael Dwyer, County Wicklow, 1798-1803", in Ken Hannigan

and William Nolan (eds.), *Wicklow: History and Society*, Dublin 1994, p. 383 and Ruán O'Donnell: *The Rebellion in Wicklow 1798,* Dublin 1998, p. 343.

3. Charles Dickson: *The life of Michael Dwyer with some account of his companions*, Dublin, 1944, p. 271 and Elaine Hoxey and Caoimhin de Lion: *Michael Dwyer – Battle of Doire na Muc*, Donard, 1988, p. 14.
4. N.A.I. 620/14/186/11.
5. N.A.I. 620/14/186/7.
6. Ruán O'Donnell: "The Rebellion of 1798 in County Wicklow" in Ken Hannigan and William Nolan (eds.), *Wicklow: History and Society*, Dublin 1994, p. 371.
7. N.A.I. 620/14/186/7.
8. Kieran Sheedy: *Upon the mercy of government*, Dublin 1988, pp. 81-123; Kieran Sheedy: *The Tellicherry Five*, Dublin 1997, pp.41-63; Charles Dickson: *The life of Michael Dwyer with some account of his companions*, Dublin, 1944, pp. 250-271.
9. N.A.I. 620/14/186/11.
10. Wicklow County Council, *Wicklow commemorating 1798-1998: Calendar of Events*, p. 19.

DWYER'S LIFE IN AUSTRALIA

MICHAEL DWYER spent twenty of his fifty-three years in Australia. Though they were eventful, it was not for these years that Dwyer is best remembered. His place in history stems from his actions during the period 1798-1803 and consequently this account of the latter part of Dwyer's life story is short. The voyage on the *Tellicherry* took Dwyer and his comrades across vast, undreamt of expanses of ocean, but it finally ended when the ship arrived at the entrance to Port Jackson on St. Valentine's Day 1806.[1] Despite initial confusion regarding the Wicklow rebels, they were each given a hundred acres of land at Cabramatta.[2] The Dwyer group may have travelled to Australia on a convict ship, but they went as free men and it seemed that a new and peaceful life awaited them in the Southern hemisphere. However, when William Bligh (famous, or rather infamous, for his role during the affair of the "Mutiny on the Bounty") succeeded Gidley King as governor of New South Wales later in 1806, the peaceable new lives of Dwyer and his comrades were threatened.[3] Bligh was paranoid about the possibility of an uprising in the colony and, considering their background, he perceived the Wicklow settlers as a huge threat. This was one instance where Dwyer's fame worked against him. Michael Dwyer was arrested as a possible ringleader of a rebellion that had not taken place and kept in solitary confinement on board the H.M.S. Porpoise.[4] Following an elaborate show trial, Dwyer was found guilty of "conspiracy in order to raise a rebellion" and in May 1807 he was sent to the convict depot on Norfolk Island.[5]

Dwyer was once again a prisoner, just as he had been in Kilmainham. He was moved from Norfolk Island to Van Dieman's Land in January 1808.[6] However, moves to oust Governor Bligh were afoot in Sydney and following the so-called "Rum Rebellion" he was removed from office.[7] With the departure of Bligh, Michael Dwyer and his companions were pardoned and released from captivity. Under the enlightened Governor Lachlan Macquarie, on 25 August 1810, Dwyer was appointed as a constable at George's River.[8] The irony of the ex-guerrilla fighter taking up such a post was not a hindrance to the growth of the Michael Dwyer legend however. Advocates of Dwyer point out that this appointment demonstrated that Dwyer had extraordinary leadership skills and that these were recognised in the raw, new, vigorous, exciting but perhaps dangerous climate of New South Wales. This was a place where "real men" were given a chance and were not stifled by the social immobility and "Ancien Regime" mentality which existed within the "old countries", now forming the "United Kingdom of Great Britain and Ireland", a political entity established by the Act of Union which came into force on 1 January 1801. By 1819 Dwyer owned six hundred and twenty acres[9] and his solid expansion of his land holding was seen as further proof of his acumen and ability. In May 1820 Dwyer was appointed Chief Constable of Liverpool and it was argued by his supporters that his rise through the system meant that he was in a better position to help other Irish emigrants-cum-convicts. Moreover, in the heady atmosphere of the raw and fledgling colony, led by the enlightened figure of Macquarie, surely men such as Dwyer had an integral part to play in the shaping of a better life for all? Dwyer the chief constable fitted very nicely into the myth as Dwyer the just, the guardian of the peace and the champion of the oppressed. Had not he fought with the United Irishmen to achieve a better quality of life for his people? Now, in a young land, albeit in a new capacity, why should he do any differently? Indeed, could he do less now than during his idealistic days of resistance back in far off Wicklow? Dwyer now served the King that he had rebelled against, but in a place where, by doing so, he could make a difference and see many of his revolutionary principles put into action.

However, the myth and the man diverge here. Dwyer had invested in a tavern called the "Harrow Inn". This was perhaps not a good move on the part of a man who was known to have a fondness for alcohol.[10] The public house brought financial problems and Dwyer was removed from his position as chief constable due to misconduct.[11] To boost his finances, Dwyer had illegally set land belonging to a woman named Ann Stroud. On Christmas Eve 1822 he was found guilty of "having broken the colonial regulations" and was fined £20. More serious however, he lost his spirit licence and was unable to pay his creditors. Many of his possessions and some of his lands were sold, and in 1824 he was incarcerated in the debtors' prison in Sydney. He was released in May 1825, but was in poor health when he returned to one of his few possessions which had not been sold – his house at Cabramatta. Weak and suffering from dysentery, he lived only another three months and the Legend died on 23 August 1825.[12]

THE FINAL RESTING PLACE

Following his death on 23 August 1825, Michael Dwyer was buried in Devonshire Street Cemetery, but in 1898 his remains were re-interred in Waverly Cemetery. A crowd of about 200,000 attended the re-interment and oral tradition states that the memorial stone is the highest of all the monuments over any Irish patriot and still the highest headstone in Sydney. Pictured at the grave are Mr. and Mrs. W. Daynes from Dunlavin parish with their grandson.

Or did it? The death of Michael Dwyer in Australia only strengthened the legend of the wronged leader who was shamefully exiled by a deceitful establishment. It was now certain that this "Exile from Erin" was "never to return". Dwyer's acceptance of the positions of constable and later chief constable was either kept hidden or worked into the myth by portraying Dwyer as a dispenser of justice for other Irish exiles. [13] Dwyer had been so well known during his guerrilla campaign and at the time of his transportation against his negotiated terms of surrender that he had achieved "celebrity status". In those pre mass media days, the press had made him into a "superstar". The longevity and Romantic nature of his mountain war had captured the imagination. Posthumously also, he became a valuable symbol – an icon – for Nationalists to aspire to and for Nationalist historians to incorporate into their corpus of literature. Although his guerrilla campaign was always peripheral to the bigger picture, the never-say-die attitude that it embodied was inspirational to a Nationalist Ireland that was crying out for heroes, and who needed those heroes to sustain its growth and development. That remarkable Glen of Imaal man Michael Dwyer was one such hero.

NOTES

1. Kieran Sheedy: *The Tellicherry Five*, Dublin 1997, p. 75.
2. Kieran Sheedy: *The Tellicherry Five*, Dublin 1997, pp. 76-80.
3. Charles Dickson: *The life of Michael Dwyer with some account of his companions*, Dublin, 1944, p. 276.
4. Kieran Sheedy: *The Tellicherry Five*, Dublin 1997, p. 88.
5. Wicklow County Council, *Wicklow commemorating 1798-1998: Calendar of Events*, p. 20.
6. Kieran Sheedy: *The Tellicherry Five*, Dublin 1997, p. 101.
7. Wicklow County Council, *Wicklow commemorating 1798-1998: Calendar of Events*, p. 20.
8. Kieran Sheedy: *The Tellicherry Five*, Dublin 1997, p. 111.
9. Kieran Sheedy: *The Tellicherry Five*, Dublin 1997, p. 121.
10. Dwyer's fondness for alcohol is well documented. Having grown up in circumstances where the shébeen was one of the principal diversions from

hardship, his arduous guerrilla campaign – particularly during the winter months – in the Wicklow Mountains almost necessitated the use of spirits. He was intoxicated on arrival in Kilmainham [Dixon, *Life*, p. 250 and Sheedy, *Government*, p. 57]. It is probable that the authorities plied him with drink in efforts to extract information. Dwyer's letter of 21 January 1805, reproduced in the previous chapter, may also suggest a dependence on spirits. In Australia, there were numerous references to his drinking [Sheedy, *Tellicherry*, pp. 123-137 passim]. The cause of Dwyer's death was given as "dysentery" and alcohol abuse is known to aggravate this condition. This note is factual, not judgemental and it must be noted that Dwyer was a product of his times.

11. Wicklow County Council, *Wicklow commemorating 1798-1998: Calendar of Events*, p. 20.
12. Kieran Sheedy: *The Tellicherry Five*, Dublin 1997, pp. 129-137.
13. Campion [*Insurgent Captain*,] wrote the Australian years almost completely out of his account of Dwyer's life, giving Dwyer's date of death as 1805. On the other hand Ronan [*Insurgent Wicklow*] mentions that Dwyer became a chief constable: *a situation of great trust. During that time he never let pass an opportunity of serving any of his countrymen who had been sent there for political offences.*

CONCLUSION

THE LIFE of Michael Dwyer was remarkable by any standards. As a young man growing up in the remote Glen of Imaal in the era of the American War of Independence and the French Revolution, there was nothing to suggest that his name and fame would echo through the centuries. Yet in many people's minds, Dwyer's name springs to mind as a defender of the "Rights of Man" much more readily than does that of Thomas Paine, the author of the celebrated pamphlet of the same name. This is due to the folk-memory aspect associated with Dwyer. Dwyer held a minor enough position within the United Irishmen before and even during the 1798 rebellion. However, his campaign in the Wicklow Mountains changed his status as a rebel and during the period 1799-1803 he became to many a major figure within the United Irish organisation. Moreover *his highly publicised escapades were an acute propaganda embarrassment for Dublin Castle.*[1]

Dwyer's escapades elevated him to the status of a hero. Although later Nationalist historians used his guerrilla campaign as a form of propaganda, they need not have exaggerated the facts of that campaign to do so. The truth was as dramatic as much of the myth. Although Dwyer's heroic status was assured at national level, nowhere was it more keenly felt than in his own area of West Wicklow. I have grown up with the legend of Michael Dwyer and the knowledge that his almost superhuman exploits happened here – in this very place. Older generations have passed on their knowledge of the great man orally. Stories were told and ballads about the Dunlavin massacre and the escape of Dwyer at Derrynamuck were sung or recited around firesides in my youth. Growing up in West Wicklow, one could not escape the sense that Michael Dwyer was a hero. It was more than a sense; it was a fact.

For me as a child, the heroic stature of the rebel leader put his memory into the realms of myth. He was the legendary Michael Dwyer – an immortal. Later examination of the historical facts of his life revealed that he was mortal after all. Far from the sentiments of T.D. Sullivan's ballad *We're true United Irishmen, we'll fight until we die,* Dwyer became a chief constable when he settled in Australia. He had shady land dealings and spent time in a debtors' prison. He drank heavily. Yes, Dwyer was mortal. He had feet of clay. Indeed, *no folk hero like Michael Dwyer could ever live up to the heroic image and the sanitised reputation which an emerging nation bestowed posthumously on him.*[2]

However, at another level, Dwyer's "feet of clay" matter not a jot. He is not remembered for his shortcomings; he is remembered for his heroism. His stout-hearted military campaign in County Wicklow was truly heroic. He did decide to fight at Derrynamuck, and whatever he may have done in later life cannot change that fact. Heroes are allowed to have feet of clay; it does not detract from their heroism. Many military heroes were fond of alcohol. In Dwyer's case, it probably dulled the pain and eased the hardship of the long-suffering leader. It certainly did nothing to detract from what was an admirable guerrilla campaign against overwhelming odds. It was this guerrilla campaign that etched Dwyer into the popular memory and modern folk-ballads continue to cement Dwyer's place in folklore. One such example is found on Andy Irvine's album "Rude Awakening".[3]

MICHAEL DWYER'S ESCAPE

Michael Dwyer is my name,
I'll not deny the same
In the mountains of West Wicklow I was born
I was in a fight of late with the men of '98
And we took Enniscorthy by storm
When the rising was put down we very quickly found
That in our own homes we could no longer dwell
But many's a lonely cave some form of comfort gave
And the people of these mountains know us well

The snow was falling fast and the night was far advanced
When the three safe houses came in view.
The weather was severe but a guard was posted near
Though the dangers on a night like this were few.
But some sneaking little spy to his master he did fly
And may I live to even up the score
For when we awoke to be sure it was no joke
To find a hundred Highland soldiers at the door

"Come out you rebel band" cried the captain in command
"For you do not have a prayer, not a hope
Surrender to me now and your lives I vow
Will be spared the bullet and the rope."
Says Dwyer to his men "Boys here we are again
Though I'm afraid this time it cannot be denied
It would take more than God's grace to defend this place
From a regiment of soldiers outside"

The house was set on fire with McAllister and Dwyer
Expecting to perish in the flames
With the powder and the smoke they were nearly overcome
Crying "A curse upon your bloody Highland games"
From behind a stable wall, a well aimed musket ball
Caused McAllister pain he could not hide
As his gun was blown away, he looked down with dismay
At his arm hanging useless by his side

He says "Dwyer I'm done, hand me up your gun
Let's see what a spring you can make"
As he opened the door he gave one loud roar
"I die for my country's sake"
The volley rang out and Dwyer sprang forth
Poor Sam received the fire
O, generous and brave McAllister gave
Up his life for Michael Dwyer

Before they could reload he was halfway down the road
With a kilted Scotsman snapping at his heels
The troopers held their fire till they saw what might transpire
And they watched as Dwyer tripped him in the field
Running like a mountain goat – no trousers, no coat
His bare feet were bleeding to be sure.
As he crossed the Black Banks he offered hearty thanks
And got safely to a cave in Glenmalure

We lost three men that day our captain got away
And the others surrendered on the spot
Three of them alas were hanged in Baltinglass
The others went to face the firing squad
Dwyer fought the law, five years, maybe more
'Til at last to Dublin he did go
And from there he set sail bound for New South Wales
Far from the County of Wicklow.

SUSTAINING THE LEGEND

Michael Dwyer's exploits live on in the folk memory of West Wicklow. The escape of Dwyer from Derrynamuck, the sacrifice of Sam McAllister at the cottage door and the deaths of Costello and Savage are all vividly depicted in this detail from a wall painting by Tadhg Phelan in "Katie Lowe's" hostelry in Kiltegan. This photograph is used courtesy of "Katie Lowe's".

Lately, in West Wicklow, where Dwyer's memory is at its most fervent, I have heard another ballad sung at local traditional sessions.[4] I do not know its origin, but the wording is as follows:

WICKLOW MEN OF NINETY-EIGHT

You Wicklow men of high renown, I'm asking for your story
Of Holt and Dwyer and many more whose names are not recorded.
Of how they fought on long and hard when all the rest had fallen,
From deep within the Wicklow hills they brought the battle forward.

In those dark days of ninety eight, the year of great rebellion,
The ghosts of men who fought back then are sitting on my shoulder
And whispering in solemn tones of how they fought with honour,
How they had tried to free our land of tyranny and murder.

How they fought Major Hardy's men, the feared Antrim Militia,
Who terrorised the county with their viciousness and cruelty;
Who'd roam at will from town to town, to burn, to rob and torture
And leave behind a trail of fear which never was forgotten.

As if this wasn't hard enough, there was the curs'd informer
Whose whispering in the darkened lanes led fine brave men to slaughter
And thinking of such valiant men as the Byrnes of Ballymanus
By a muttered word of a craven cur, such men were taken from us.

So, Wicklow men of high renown, I'm asking for your story
Of Holt and Dwyer and many more whose names are not recorded.

Dwyer's name was recorded and the tales of his exploits have survived the man himself. His memory lives on and his place in Irish history is assured. Stories, songs and ballads have all contributed to the legend of Michael Dwyer. They have also contributed to the popular knowledge of the man behind the myth. It is my sincere hope that this little volume will do likewise.

CHRIS LAWLOR,
Dunlavin,
January 2003.

NOTES

1. Kevin Whelan: *Fellowship of Freedom: The United Irishmen and 1798*, Cork, 1998, p. 105.
2. Kieran Sheedy: *Upon the mercy of government*, Dublin 1988, p. 263.
3. Website: http://www.dwyerclan.com/Michael_Dwyers_Escape.htm visited on 1/7/2002. Andy Irvine's album is available in the U.S.A. on Greenlinnet Records and may be purchased on the internet at http://www.greenlinnet.com/shopping/
4. I am indebted to Mrs. Maureen Downey of Dunlavin for the words of this song, of which she sings an excellent version. Incidentally, her husband, Mr. Liam Downey, also gives a fine rendition of the ballad "Dunlavin Green". Sincere thanks to you both.

Appendices

APPENDIX ONE: THE DUNLAVIN MASSACRE

THE BALLAD DUNLAVIN GREEN

The standard form of this ballad, as published in Matthew Hodgart (ed.), **The Faber Book of Ballads** (London 1965) on page 202 is as follows:

DUNLAVIN GREEN
In the year of one thousand seven hundred and ninety eight,
A sorrowful tale the truth unto you I'll relate.
Of thirty-six heroes to the world were left to be seen,
By a false information were shot on Dunlavin Green.

Bad luck to you, Saunders, for you did their lives betray;
You said a parade would be held on that very day,
Our drums they did rattle - our fifes they did sweetly play;
Surrounded we were and privately marched away.

Quite easy they led us as prisoners through the town,
To be slaughtered on the plain, we then were forced to kneel down,
Such grief and such sorrow were never before there seen,
When the blood ran in streams down the dykes of Dunlavin Green.

There is young Matty Farrell, has plenty of cause to complain,
Also the two Duffys, who were shot down on the plain,
And young Andy Ryan, his mother distracted will run
For her own brave boy, her beloved eldest son.

Bad luck to you, Saunders, bad luck may you never shun!
That the widow's curse may melt you like snow in the sun,

The cries of the orphans whose murmurs you cannot screen,
For the murder of their dear fathers, on Dunlavin Green.

Some of our boys to the hills they are going away,
Some of them are shot, and some of them going to sea,
Micky Dwyer in the mountains to Saunders he owes a spleen,
For his loyal brothers, who were shot on Dunlavin Green.

The White Collection in the **Library of Trinity College**, Dublin also contains the following version of the ballad:

A LAMENTATION ON THE HEROES WHO WERE SHOT ON DUNLAVIN GREEN

In the year of one thousand seven hundred and ninety eight
A sorrowful ditty to you I am going to relate
Concerning those heroes both clever and rare to be seen
By false information were shot upon Dunlavin green.

Woe to you Saunders, disgrace me you never shall
That the tears of the widows may melt you like snow before the sun;
Those fatherless orphans! Their cries nor moans can't be screened,
For the loss of their fathers, who were shot upon Dunlavin Green.

Some of our heroes are 'listed and gone far away,
There are some of them dead, and some of them crossing the sea;
As for poor Andy Ryan, his mother distracted has been
For the loss of her son, who was shot upon Dunlavin Green.

As for Andy Farrell, I'm sure he has cause to complain
And likewise the two Duffys, I'm sure they may well do the same;
Dwyer on the mountain, to the orange he owes a great spleen,
For the loss of his comrades, who were shot upon Dunlavin Green.

They were marched from the guard house up to the end of the town,
And when they came there the poor fellows were forced to kneel down,
Like lambs for the slaughter that day it was plain to be seen,
Their blood ran in streams on the dykes of Dunlavin Green.

That we may live happy the joyful tidings to hear ,
When we will have satisfaction for the murders they did in that year;
There were thirty-six heroes, both clever and rare to be seen,
Both Loyal and United, shot one day on Dunlavin Green.

Now to conclude, and finish my mournful tale,
I hope all good Christians to pray for their souls will not fail.
Their souls in white pigeons, a-flying to heaven were seen
On the very same day they were shot upon Dunlavin Green.

The Shearman Papers in the **Russell Library, N.U.I. Maynooth** also contain an alternative version of the ballad:

DUNLAVIN GREEN
Of the year seventeen hundred and ninety-eight,
A sorrowful ditty and I am going to relate:
Of thirty-six heroes whose like were never seen,
Who by false information were shot on Dunlavin Green.

They were marched from the market house and up through the town
And coming to the green they were ordered to kneel down.
Oh such horror and such terror, the like were never seen,
When those heroes lay bleeding in the dykes of Dunlavin Green.

When the sad news came to each village and each town,
Some were a sowing and more were a mowing
And more were following the ploughs,
While their wives were a spinning and milking the cows.

They gave up the sowing and mowing and creeping stealthily along,
Their briars and their ditches and leaping o'er walls so strong,
They came to the green and to their grief were seen
The heroes lying in their gore in the dykes of Dunlavin Green.

I am sure Nancy Ryan has reason to complain,
And the two late Duffys can in sorrow do the same,
And Mat Byrne whose fine son distracted had he been
At the slaughter of the heroes shot on Dunlavin Green.

My curse on you Saunders, bad luck may you never shun,
May the tears of widows and orphans melt you like the snow before the sun,
May poverty and sorrow on you and yours be seen
For the slaughter of those heroes in the dykes of Dunlavin Green.

The Executed Men.
The names of thirty-six men who were shot on the fairgreen are given in Chris Lawlor, **The Massacre on Dunlavin Green – A Story of the 1798 Rebellion** (Naas 1998) on pages 98-99. They are as follows:

YEOMEN – SAUNDERSGROVE CORPS:

1. James Mara (Maher)
2. John Williams
3. Andrew Ryan
4. Patrick Duffy
5. James Duffy

6. John Webb
7. Patrick Curran
8. David Lee
9. Mat Kavanagh
10. Richard Kelly
11. Morgan Doyle
12. Thomas Doyle
13. Mat Farrell
14. James Moran
15. Charles Evers
16. William Dwyer
17. Thomas Brien
18. David Prendergast

YEOMEN – NARRAGHMORE CORPS:

19. James Keating
20. Thomas Keating
21. Martin Walsh
22. Edward Shaughnessy
23. Andrew Carty
24. Darby Byrne
25. John Dunne
26. Martin Griffin
27. Daniel Kirwam
28. Thomas Kirwan
29. Laurence Doyle
30. Thomas Neile

LOCAL MEN FROM DUNLAVIN PARISH

31. John Dwyer, Seskin
32. Peter Hayden, Imaal (Keadeen)
33. Peter Kearney, Donard
34. Laurence Doyle, Dunlavin

ALSO 35. John Brien
36. Joe Hawkins

The **Shearman Papers** also names thirty of the victims of that day:

1. John Keeravan, {Brothers of Uppertown, Dunlavin.
2. Daniel Keeravan { This surname was printed as 'Reeravan' in *The Sham Squire.*
3. Laurence Doyle, Dunlavin.
4. Martin Gryffin (at 21 he came from Dublin the night before to see his father and was not connected with United men).
5. Duffy {Brothers of
6. Duffy {Baltinglass.
7. Mathew Farrell, Stratford on Slaney.
8. Michael Neil [Dunlavin].
9. Andrew Ryan, Shrucka.
10. Richard Williams, Ballinacrow.
11. Keatinge {of Narraghmore
12. Keatinge {[brothers].
13. Edward Slattery, Narraghmore .
14. Andrew Prendergast of Ballina?
15. Peter Kearney, Donard.
16. John Dwyer do, uncle to Capt. Michael Dwyer.
17. John Kearney, Donard.
18. Peter Headon, Killabeg.
19. Thomas Brien, Ballinacrow Hill.
20. John Doyle, Scrughawn.
21. Morgan Doyle, Tuckmill, Baltinglass.
22. John Doyle do.
23. Webb, Baltinglass.
24. John Wickham, Eadestown.
25. Wickham do.
26. Costelloe.
27. Bermingham {Brothers of Narraghmore,
28. Bermingham {belonging to Col. Keatinge's corps.

29. Patrick Moran, Tuckmill.
30. Peter Prendergast of Bumbo Hall, wounded in the belly and escaped.

Shearman provides extra names for victims, and given the fact that so many sources are so definite that thirty-six men were shot, I presume that the other victims were hanged at the market house – after the massacre, according to Shearman ' s account.

Thirty-six names were given in **Massacre on Dunlavin Green**. Fr. Shearman names thirty of the victims that day, obviously with some degree of overlap. The total number of named victims now rises to fifty-two allowing for different Christian names, but some (e.g. Peter Prendergast here and David Prendergast above) are obviously the same man. However it seems safe to assume that the death toll in the village that day must be revised to a figure somewhere in the mid-forties at least.

APPENDIX TWO: COURTS-MARTIAL RECORDS

Proceedings of a General Court Martial held at Baltinglass on the 19th February 1799 by order of his Excellency the Lord Lieutenant.

President: Captain Bellock, Dumfries Lt. Dragoons. Members: Captain Blood, Clare Militia; Captain Jackson, ditto; Lieut. Eames, ditto; Lieut. De Renzy, Wicklow Militia; Lieut. Comyns, Clare Militia; Lieut. Drew, ditto; Cornet Shaw, Dumfries Lt. D; Ensign Whitedown, Clare Militia; Ensign England, Acting Judge Advocate.

Michael Doyle for rebellion, robbery and murder.

James Whelan the evidence against the prisoner having suffered death in pursuance of his Excellency's warrant, here follows the affidavit sworn by him before his death and was sworn it enclosed.

Prisoner's defence:
Michael Doyle denies whole.

Sentence: The court having considered the evidence contained in the affidavit sworn by James Whelan before his death are of opinion that Michael Doyle is guilty and do therefore sentence him to be transported for life.
C. Bellock, Captain Dumfries Lt. D. and President

County of Wicklow To Wit:
James Whelan of Fryenstown in said county being duly sworn on the Holy Evangelists and examined, said that on the evening of the 22nd of December last he went to the house of James Hughes of Stratford with John Riley of Wine Tavern and Michael Doyle of Stratford and the said Michael Doyle asked the defendant to accompany him towards Manger Bridge along the road with J. Reilly, that the said Michael Doyle after they came part of the way, pulled out from below his coat a short gun and bayonet and that Reilly had a pistol, that Michael Doyle informed the defendant that he was going to rob Farrel Doyle, that he thought it reasonable to rob him as after the battle of Stratford

he would not give him a night's lodging or any other substance; that the said Farrel Doyle had a good quantity of bacon and money, that his wife had three rings and a pair of silver buckles, that said Michael Doyle gave this deponent the pistol and the bayonet and desired him to go into the said house and told him to say that they came from Captain [Michael] Dwyer and that he and those with him were sent to burn the houses of James Valentine, Patrick Price and Mrs. Valentine and that if he did not behave like a stout fellow the said Michael Doyle swore he would shoot him; that the said Michael Doyle said he would not enter the house least he should be known; that the said Michael Doyle desired to give the said Farrel Doyle some stabs of the bayonet if he did not give him money. The deponent then rapped at the door of Farrel Doyle's house which he entered and told the said Farrel Doyle that there were some men at the door who wanted money and after some conversation he took a guinea and half a crown which he took out to the said John Riley and Michael Doyle. The said Michael Doyle snatched the gun from Riley and asked the deponent how much he had got. When the deponent told them Riley said he was "too soft" and the said Michael Doyle swore violently he would shoot him if he did not go in again and take the three rings and ten guineas and desired the deponent to put all the people of the house into the room until he would go in for the bacon and also desired the deponent to get shirts etc; that the deponent went in and requested Mrs. Doyle to conceal her rings and buckles as he was not willing to take them. When the deponent went out of the house, said Riley told him that he had entered the house and taken out the bacon and made the deponent assist to carry part of it up Manger Hill. The said Michael Doyle took two parts of the said bacon and Riley one which the said Riley took home with him to Randalstown to the back of his father's house and the said Michael Doyle took his part down the road towards Manger Bridge using the precaution of stripping off his coat lest it should be soiled with it. That the said Mrs. Doyle's petticoat was taken by Riley and a pair of stockings which the deponent took from Mrs. Doyle of which the said Michael Doyle and John Riley took one stocking each. That the said Michael Doyle told the deponent that he was one of the persons along with Michael Kehoe who before robbed said Farrel Doyle of money and clothes of all sorts and not short of as much as would make him up forever. That said things he found concealed in a tub or chest barrel in an outhouse belonging to Farrel Doyle and that the boy who then lived with him knew how things were situated in the house. The said Kehoe had his plunder stored in his house under the ash, and wanted the said Whelan to go with him and take them from the said Kehoe on the night of the 6th January inst. The deponent was sick having recently too much and the said Michael Doyle went from him towards Farrel Doyle's, stayed some little time and returned with Riley and charged the deponent with having dropped some words in the town of Stratford about his former robbery of Farrel Doyle that if he was convinced of it he would instantly go to [Original torn] and asked him to now own to [Original torn] towards which in a ditch the deponent attempted to stoop down to hide a watch and pocket book. The said Michael Doyle made a violent thrust at him with a bayonet, which was fixed on a fork and short handle with two iron rings and which he drew through the thigh of the said deponent and then called out to John Riley to fire at him which he attempted to do but his pistol missed fire. Whelan ran from them and made his escape. The deponentnt further says that he heard the said Michael Doyle and John Riley say that they and a Curtis Doyle of Randalstown were the persons who attempted to rob the office of Messrs. Orrs of Stratford in November last and would have effectively done so had it not been for the cowardice of the men who stood frightened, who called them off before they could break open the only door which they to effect to come at the money, as they thought.

James Whelan before me this day 11th day of January 1799.

Morley Saunders

Examined – bound in the sum of fifty pounds still to appear and prosecute at the next assizes... 19th February 1799

MILITARY BASTION OF WEST WICKLOW

Baltinglass was the nerve-centre of martial law within the region and many prisoners were held in captivity in the town before being court-martialled. This wall-plaque commemorates all those who were killed during both the rebellion and Dwyer's prolonged military resistance afterwards.

Proceeding of General Court Martial held at Baltinglass March 9th by order of his Excellency the Lord Lieutenant.

President: Captain Bellock, Drumfries Lt. Dragoons. Members: Captain Blood, Clare Militia; Lieut. Bridgeman, ditto; Lieut Eames, ditto; Lieut. De Renzy, Wicklow Militia; Lieut. Morrice, Clare Militia; Lieut. Comyns, ditto; Cornet Shaw, Dumfries Lt. Dragoons; Ensign White-down, Clare Militia; Ensign England, Acting Judge Advocate.

James Comyns for rebellion and robbing Michael Fenton a yeoman of his arms, ammunition and accoutrements and making for the hills with said articles.

Michael Fenton sworn is a Yeoman in the Dunlavin Corps of Yeomanry. The prisoner lived in his house and in October last, he one night stole witness's arms, ammunition and accoutrements, viz. a musket and a bayonet, a cartridge box with fifteen rounds, broadsword and helmet, regimental coat and waistcoat. Witness hearing three weeks ago that the prisoner had been taken by a party of the Glengarry Fencibles at Radangan near Hacketstown, went there, saw the prisoner and identified his arms and accoutrements which he still had on when taken. The arms etc. were produced before the Court and Michael Fenton's name found written in the inside of the coat and waistcoat. He swore the arms etc. were his own and the same the prisoner had run away with.

Prisoner in his defence said that he had drunk too much whiskey and that he had committed the robbery in a fit of insobriety.

The Court having duly and maturely considered the evidence for and against the prisoner James Comyns are unanimously of opinion that he is guilty of the crime laid to his charge and do therefore sentence him to death.

Sentence: Death Confirmed

C. Bellock, Captain Dumfries Lt. D. President.
[Jotted in afterwards]
Approved – Cornwallis.
Baltinglass No. 10
General Court Martial of J. Comyns 9th March '99.

Proceedings of a General Court Martial held at Baltinglass, March 13th by order of his Excellency, the Lord Lieutenant.

President: Captain Bellock (Dumfries Lt. Dragoons). Members: Captain Blood, Clare Militia; Lieut. Bridgeman, ditto; Lieut. Morrice, ditto; Lieut Eames, ditto; Lieut. De Renzy, WicklowMilitia; Lieut. Comyns, ditto; Cornet Shaw, Dumfries Lt. Dragoons; Ensign Whitedown; Clare

Militia; Ensign England, Acting Judge Advocate.

Prisoner: **John Byrns** for Rebellion and carrying arms against His Majesty's forces.

Joseph Hawkins sworn is a yeoman in the Honourable Captain Stratford's corps, went out with a party in October last to the Glen of Emale where many houses had been burnt by the rebels. Said Party came up with some of the rebels, prisoner was among them and witness had known him a long time before. After some shots had been exchanged the rebels ran away, the prisoner himself was pursued by witness and some other yeomen. Prisoner ran into a boggy ground and leapt over a large ditch and then fired his piece at the yeomen, who, being on horseback, could not follow him in the bog. Prisoner got clear off and carried his arms with him. Witness hearing that prisoner had been taken by a party of the Glengarry Fencibles, went to Hacketstown and identified him. Witness swore that prisoner was the man who fired at him in the Glen of Emale.

James Fenton sworn is a yeoman in Captain Hume's corps, was out with the party that went in October last to the Glen of Emale under the command of Lieutenant Downy of the 89th Regiment. The party fell in with the rebels in the Glen and put them to fright. Witness corroborates the evidence given by Joseph Hawkins and was himself fired at by the prisoner after he had cleared the ditch.

Lawrence Doyle sworn is a servant of Lieutenant Fenton of Mr. Hume's corps, was driving a cart loaded with leather belonging to his master in November last. He was met by the prisoner who was armed with a musket and who asked him whose leather it was? Witness said it was Mr. Fenton's. Prisoner then said he did not want the leather, but that if the "rascally Orange-man" (his master) was ever in his way, he should sell leather no more. Mr. Fenton is a leather merchant.

Prisoner acknowledged the truth of the evidence and begged to be transported to any of His Majesty's Dominions.

Sentence: The Court having duly and maturely considered the evidence for and against the prisoner, John Byrns, are unanimously of opinion that he is guilty of rebelliously carrying arms against his majesty's troops and do therefore sentence him to death.

C. Bellock, Captain Dumfries Lt. Dragoons. President.

[Jotted in afterwards]
Approved – Cornwallis.
Baltinglass No.15
Trial of John Byrns for Rebellion 13th March 1799.

Proceedings of a General Court Martial held at Baltinglass 22nd December 1800 by virtue of an order from his Excellency the Lord Lieutenant of which Lt. Colonel Hugh Dive of the D.Y.R. is President.

Members: Captain Alan Cobban, D.Y.R. Highland Regiment; Captain John Feeny, D.Y.R. Highland Regiment; Lieut. John Gibson, D.Y.R. Highland Regiment; Lieut. George MacKenzie, Caithness Legion.

The President, members of the Court and Captain Robert Grant, D.Y.R. Highlanders acting Judge Advocate duly sworn proceeded to identify **William Genoud.**

The Judge advocate having read the proceedings of a Court Martial on the prisoner Genoud and others held at Baltinglass on the 6th November 1798. The sentence of which adjudged they suffer death by being hanged and having demanded of the prisoner what he had to say in defence and why that sentence should not now be put in execution. The prisoner acknowledged himself to be William Genoud and that he was the same person tried by the foresaid court martial, but says that after he escaped from the Guard House he got a protection from the Honourable Captain Stratford and remained between three and four months at his house until he was driven from it by some yeomen.

The Honourable Captain Stratford being sworn deposes that he did write a note to Genoud saying that he would endeavour to obtain his pardon provided he would give useful information, as he understood he could discover where many arms were concealed.That the deponent wrote Government in his favour and got an answer to say that if the prisoner made these discoveries the recommendation would be attended to; that the deponent told the prisoner's wife of the above terms intimating to her that if the prisoner did not by a certain day came forward and made such discovery that he would consider the protection withdrawn, and says the prisoner did not come in nor make any discovery whatever.

Captain King being sworn.

Question by the prisoner: Whether some time after he escaped from the Guard House if he remembered the prisoner's wife applying to him to know why her husband was pursued having Captain Stratford's protection?

Captain King says he did not, but would enquire of Captain Stratford: Answer: He did remember her asking him such a question was his answer.

Robert Grant
Acting as Judge Advocate.

H. Dive. Lt. Colonel, President.

Proceedings of a Court Marital held at Baltinglass on 22nd December 1800 to identify Mander or Genoud.

Sentence: Death.
Warrant drawn the 24th December 1800.

Additional Memorandum

Memorandum of what passed between the prisoner Genoude and

Ensign Nicholson, Aide de Camp, Baltinglass. 15th December 1800.

I asked Genoud if he could say anything in his justification or if he could say or do anything that might incline the Government to extend mercy to him. He replied that he could not say anything in his defence, that the crimes he was guilty of he was told deserved death, but that there were great numbers out who deserved it more than he did, that he could not now say, or do, anything that would incline Government to extend mercy to him.

I was, when leaving Baltinglass followed by Genoude's wife who told me that if he was removed from Baltinglass to one of the neighbouring prisons he would give valuable information.

Joseph Nicolson, Aide de Camp.

Horse hire and expenses in Baltinglass for Edward Dowling, Richard Kirwan, Christopher Bently and John Taylor, it being unsafe for them to return last night: £0-19s-6d.

Mr. Patterson's Letter

Dublin 18th December 1800.

Sir,

I had the honour to receive your letter communicating to me His Excellency's commands that I should point out specifically the steps necessary to be taken in the case of William Noude or Genoude in consequence of the several papers and documents transmitted to me, all of which I herewith return.

You will please to inform His Excellency that in my opinion a Court Martial should be ordered to assemble, before which Noude or Genoude should be brought a prisoner. The person acting as advocate general should have the proceedings of the Court Martial which tried Noude or Genoude in his hands and lay them before the Court. He should then call on Noude or Genoude and state to him that at a Court Martial heretofore held at Baltinglass, stating the time from the proceedings, he had been tried for the crimes stated in the proceedings, setting them forth that he had been found guilty thereof; that sentence of death and execution thereon had adjudged and awarded against him which judgement could not since be carried into execution in consequence of his having broken out of prison; then to demand of him if he has anything to say why judgement of death and execution thereon should not now be awarded against him agreeable to the sentence before passed. It is probable he will confess himself to be the same person who was before tried, if so the Court will record it; if not his identity must be proved by calling on Lieutenant Rawson and any other of the persons mentioned in the same information with him, which must likewise be recorded if so found or a contra.

If his identity is found, a warrant I think may then issue for his execution.

This I humbly beg leave to submit is the regular and proper mode of proceeding on the present occasion.

I have etc.
Francis Patterson.
Col. Littlehales.

APPENDIX THREE: DWYERS OF CUMNOCK WEBSITE

The Dwyers of Cumnock

as narrated by

Michael DWYER, Cumnock, April 1997

The DWYERs are political refugees from County Wicklow in Ireland. The progenitor of the Australian line of DWYERs are Michael DWYER and Mary DOYLE who emigrated to Australia. Michael was known as the 'Wicklow Chief of the Glen', and his wife Mary the 'Queen of the Mountains' after leading the fighting against the British rule in Ireland.

Michael was born in 1772 in the townland of Camara, the eldest of the seven children of John DWYER and Mary BYRNE of County Wicklow. He grew up under the political influence of the United Irishmen, and was one of the ring leaders of the Rebellion of 1798. After much fighting in the mountains of the County, he negotiated a surrender and was exiled to Australia. He arrived in Port Jackson with nine other exiles on 15 February 1806 on the '*Tellicherry*'. His children born in Ireland never saw him again, arriving in Australia not long after his death which occurred on 23 August 1825. The seven children of his marriage to Mary DOYLE are:

Maryanne	b. 1799 Wicklow
John	b. 1801 Wicklow
Peter	b. 1802 Wicklow
Esther	b. 1804 Wicklow
James	b. 1806 NSW
Bridget	b. 1808 Tasmania
Elizabeth	b. 1812 NSW

After Michael's death, his wife Mary and daughters Bridget and Eliza worked as housekeepers in Sydney for the high profile Father John Joseph Therry. The rest of the family joined them from Ireland in

1828. Mary died in June 1860, and was buried with Michael in the Devonshire St. Cemetery in Sydney.

In 1898, the centenery of the Rebellion, their bodies were exhumed and laid to rest in the magnificent marble '1798 Irish Memorial' in Waverley Cemetery. The memorial service in St Mary's Cathedral, and the procession to the cemetery was attended by thousands.

It was their son Peter who settled in Bathurst and married Mary Darley WHITE in 1831. They had six children, including two boys, Michael Robert, (a bachelor who died in Dubbo district) and John Edward. It is believed that later in life Peter formed a liaison with Bridget Ellen "Granny" BROWN, who was the mother of Michael DWYER born around 1857. The exact history is not known as to the relationships between Peter and these two women. Peter eventually moved to Bungendore and owned 'The Palms' property and at one stage owned the local Hotel. His brother John had already settled in the area.

Peter DWYER died on 5 Nov 1876, and is buried at Bungendore, near Canberra. Granny BROWN died on 18 October 1907, aged 75 years, and is buried at Cumnock.

It was Michael DWYER and his mother who selected "Glendale" in the 1860's, and this property remains in the DWYER family to this date, now owned by John DWYER, grandson of the above Michael. The property is now 812 acres in size.

Michael married Isabella LEWIS on 5 Nov 1882. Isabella was a servant girl working in Cumnock at the time. She was one of three children of the marriage of Joseph LEWIS, a cab proprietor of Sydney, and a native of London. His parents were Joseph LEWIS and Esther HUMPHREY, shopkeepers of London. At the time of his marriage in 1857 in Sydney to Catherine Malone, a native of County Kildare in Ireland, Joseph LEWIS was 53 years of age. Catherine was about 25 years old then, and working as a servant at the time. They lived in Church St.,

Parramatta, and were married in Scots Presbyterian Church, Church Hill, Sydney. Her parents were Patrick MALONE and Elizabeth NEAL. It is not known how and when either Joseph LEWIS or Catherine MALONE arrived in Australia.

One child of the marriage of Joseph LEWIS and Catherine MALONE was Joseph, who married Kate ARROW. They had three children George, Leslie and Jessie. George was a natural sportsman, an excellent shot, and became a professional boxer with the Sharman troupe before joining the Queensland Police Force. He was based in Cunnamulla when he was severely bashed by a gang of local natives. George eventually died of cancer in October 1963, aged 65 years. His mother Kate ARROW is buried at Cunnamulla.

The other child of the marriage is Isabella, who married Michael DWYER. It is believed that there was a third child Louisa. The children of the marriage of Michael DWYER and Isabella LEWIS are:

James 'Jim'	m. Maggie McNAMARA, lived in Camperdown
Catherine 'Kit'	m. Bert HART
Martin	m. Clare DURR
Bridget	**m. Jim McKEON of "Boxfield Park"**
Claude	m. Mary 'Daphne' JOHNSTON
John 'Jack'	m. Minerva ROGERS late in life

Jim was the eldest boy, and Jack the youngest. Their mother Isobella died when Claude was about 9 or 10 years of age ie., about 1910. Claude and Daphne were married on 11 June 1923 and had 5 children, some of whom still reside in Cumnock and Orange:

Isobell	b. 1924	John	b. 1934
Lola	b. 1925	Patsy	b. 1936
Michael	b. 1932		

***Bibliography**: The best reference works of the Dwyer family in Ireland and Australia is 'The Rebel of Glenmalure, A History of Michael Dwyer' by George Cargeeg, published by Hesperian Press, PO Box 317 Victoria Park, Western Australia.*

Return to The McKeon Family History. This page last updated 7 June 1997.

All text and graphics prepared by Joe Slaven

APPENDIX FOUR

The Michael Dwyer Bicentennial Commemoration Committee

Chairperson: Tommy Cullen M.C.C.
Vice Chairperson: Pat Doran M.C.C.
Secretary: Finbarr Coyle.
Treasurer: Harry Murphy.
P.R.O.: Bill Walshe.
Sculptor: Paddy Roe.
Artistic Advisor: Eve Carroll.
Fundraising Officer: Jim Keogh.
Local Advisor: Seán Byrne
Historical Advisor: Chris Lawlor M.A., H.D.E.
Special Appreciation to the late Jim Rogers *for his input.*

Monument Construction

Draughtsman: Vincent Cronin.
Contractor: Pat O'Neill and 'Parnell Construction' Crew.
Stonemason: Jack Corcoran and Team.

Special Thanks to the following

Site donated by: Harry Murphy and Family.
Religious Service by: Fr. Paddy Finn P.P. Dunlavin, Donard and Davidstown.
Calligraphy by: Olivia and Jacinta Walshe.

Sponsors

Wicklow County Council.
Wicklow Rural Partnership.
Department of Defence and Staff of Coolmooney Camp.
Dublin Products, Dunlavin.
Quinn's of Baltinglass.
Keatley Concrete.

SELECT BIBLIOGRAPHY

GENERAL WORKS

1. Sean Cronin and Richard Roche, *Freedom the Wolfe Tone Way*, Tralee 1973.
2. William Fitzpatrick: *The Sham Squire and the Informers of 1798*, Dublin 1866.
3. Daniel Gahon, *The People's Rising: Wexford 1798*, Dublin 1995.
4. Michael Kenny, The 1798 Rebellion: *Photographs and memorabilia from the National Museum of Ireland*, Dublin 1996.
5. Frank MacDermot, *Tone and his times,* Tralee 1969.
6. R.R. Madden: *Literary Remains of the United Irishmen of 1798 and selections from other popular lyrics of their times*, Dublin, 1887.
7. Sean McMahon: *Robert Emmet*, Cork, 2001.
8. Thomas Pakenham, *The Year of Liberty*, London 1972.
9. Patrick C. Power, *The Courts Martial of 1798*, Carlow 1997.
10. Kevin Whelan, *Fellowship of Freedom: The United Irishmen and 1798,* Cork 1998.

WORKS ON THE WICKLOW-CARLOW AREA

1. Carlow County Council/Carlow Urban District Council: *Carlow '98 Bicentenary Commemoration 1798-1998: Schedule of Events.*
2. Claude Chavasse: *The Story of Baltinglass*, Kilkenny Journal Ltd. 1970.
3. L.M. Cullen, "Politics and Rebellion – Wicklow in the 1790s" in Ken Hannigan and William Nolan (eds), *Wicklow: History and Society*, Dublin 1994.
4. Robert Duffy, *One hundred years too soon: Hacketstown and 1798*, Hacketstown Community Council, 1998.
5. Deirdre Heaney: *Land and Life in the Glen of Imaal 1830-1901*, Unpublished B.A. Thesis, N.U.I. Maynooth 1983.
6. Chris Lawlor: *Canon Frederick Donovan's Dunlavin 1884-1896: A West Wicklow Village in the Late Nineteenth Century*, Dublin 2000.
7. Chris Lawlor, "Dunlavin Green Revisited" in *Dunlavin-Donard-Davidstown Parish Link,* Vol. IV, No. 3, November 1998.
8. Chris Lawlor: "From Wicklow to Woomera – Wicklow's Criminal Australian Connections" in *Dunlavin Festival of Arts Brochure*, XVI, Dunlavin.
9. Chris Lawlor: "Loose Ends from the Dunlavin Area 1797-1803" in *Dunlavin Festival of Arts Brochure*, XVIII, Naas 2000.

10. Chris Lawlor, *The Massacre on Dunlavin Green – A Story of the 1798 Rebellion*, Naas 1998.
11. Chris Lawlor: "Unfinished Business" in *Dunlavin-Donard-Davidstown Parish Link,* Vol.V, No. 1, July 1999.
12. Samuel Russell McGee: *Dunlavin, County Wicklow – A Retrospect*, Dublin 1935.
13. Patrick O'Byrne: "West Wicklow" in *Souvenir Guide and Programme of the Imaal Bazaar and Fete,* Leinster Leader Ltd. Naas, 1926.
14. Ruán O'Donnell: *Aftermath: Post-Rebellion Insurgency in Wicklow 1799-1803,* Dublin 1999.
15. Ruán O Donnell: *Exploring Wicklow's Rebel Past 1798-1803*, Wicklow 1998.
16. Ruán O'Donnell: *The Rebellion in Wicklow 1798,* Dublin 1998.
17. Ruán O'Donnell: "The Rebellion of 1798 in County Wicklow" in Ken Hannigan and William Nolan (eds.), *Wicklow: History and Society*, Dublin 1994.
18. Ruán O'Donnell, "Ultra-Loyalism in Wicklow: The case of the Dunlavin massacre" in *Wicklow Historical Society Journal,* Vol. 2, No. 4, May 1998.
19. Pat Power: *People of Wicklow 1798*, Dun Laoghaire 1999.
20. Pat Power, "The Battle of Arklow" in *Wicklow Historical Society Journal,* Vol. 2, No. 4, May 1998.
21. Myles V. Ronan (ed.), *Insurgent Wicklow 1798*, Dublin 1948.
22. Wicklow County Council, *Wicklow commemorating 1798-1998: Calendar of Events.*

WORKS ON DWYER

1. Thomas Bartlett, "Masters of the mountains: the insurgent careers of Joseph Holt and Michael Dwyer, County Wicklow, 1798-1803", in Ken Hannigan and William Nolan (eds.), *Wicklow: History and Society*, Dublin 1994.
2. John Thomas Campion*: Michael Dwyer or the insurgent captain of the Wicklow Mountains: A tale of the rising in 1798*, Glasgow, no date.
3. Con Costello: "Michael Dwyer in Captivity" in *Journal of the West Wicklow Historical Society*, II, 1985/1986.
4. Charles Dickson: *The life of Michael Dwyer with some account of his companions*, Dublin, 1944.
5. Elaine Hoxey and Caoimhin de Lion: *Michael Dwyer – Battle of Doire na Muc*, Donard, 1988.
6. Paul Gorry, "The Family of Michael Dwyer" in *Journal of the West Wicklow Historical Society*, I, 1983-1984.
7. Kieran Sheedy: *The Tellicherry Five*, Dublin 1997.
8. Kieran Sheedy: *Upon the mercy of government*, Dublin 1988.

WEB PAGES

There are many web pages with a Dwyer connection. The following is just a small selection.

1. http://members.ozemail.com.au/~slaven01/mckeon/dwyer.html
2. http://members.tripod.com/granitefields/new_page_3.htm
3. http://omega.cc.umb.edu/~irish/october_1998.html
4. http://www.bartleby.com/224/0922.html
5. http://www.dwyerclan.com/Three_Flowers.htm
6. http://www.iol.ie/~walshpa/mdwyer.html
7. http://www.linuxlots.com/~dunne/ireland/Michael_Dwyer.html
8. http://www.local.ie/general/history/1798/biog.shtml
9. http://www.waverley.nsw.gov.au/library/about/historical/cm_wlk_6.htm

MANUSCRIPTS, DOCUMENTS AND NEWSPAPERS

1. National Archives, Bishop Street, Dublin, *The Rebellion Papers* 620 Series
2. National Archives, Bishop Street, Dublin, *Wicklow Gaol Register*
3. National Library, Kildare Street, Dublin, *The Cullen Papers*
4. Russell Library, N.U.I. Maynooth, *The Shearman Papers*, VII and XVII
5. Trinity College Library, Special Collections, *The White Collection*
6. The 'Freeman's Journal'.
7. The 'Leinster Leader'.
8. The 'Press'.
9. The 'Wicklow People'.

ORAL TRADITION

I am indebted to the people of my own place, West Wicklow, both living and dead, for the way in which they have kept the tradition of Michael Dwyer alive over time. I extend my sincere thanks to each and every one of them.